Britain in the
European Community

London: H M S O

Researched and written by Reference Services, Central Office of Information.

This publication is an expanded and updated version of a booklet with the same title previously published by the Foreign & Commonwealth Office.

ISBN 0 11 701712 4

HMSO publications are available from:
HMSO Publications Centre
(Mail, fax and telephone orders only)
PO Box 276, London SW8 5DT
Telephone orders 071-873 9090
General enquiries 071-873 0011
(queuing system in operation for both numbers)
Fax orders 071-873 8200

HMSO Bookshops
49 High Holborn, London WC1V 6HB   071-873 0011
Fax 071-873 8200 (counter service only)
258 Broad Street, Birmingham B1 2HE   021-643 3740   Fax 021-643 6510
Southey House, 33 Wine Street, Bristol BS1 2BQ
0272 264306   Fax 0272 294515
9-21 Princess Street, Manchester M60 8AS   061-834 7201   Fax 061-833 0634
16 Arthur Street, Belfast BT1 4GD   0232 238451   Fax 0232 235401
71 Lothian Road, Edinburgh EH3 9AZ   031-228 4181   Fax 031-229 2734
HMSO's Accredited Agents
(see Yellow Pages)
and through good booksellers

Photo Credits

Numbers refer to the pages of the illustration section (1–4): Reuters/Bettman, New York p. 1 (bottom); QA Photos: copyright The Channel Tunnel Group Limited p. 3 (top and bottom); Donald Cooper p. 4 (top).

Contents

Introduction

Britain[1] is an active and committed member of the European Community, an association of 12 nations which also comprises Belgium, Denmark, France, Germany, Greece, the Irish Republic, Italy, Luxembourg, the Netherlands, Portugal and Spain.

Britain regards the Community as a means of strengthening democracy and reinforcing political stability in Europe, of developing a thriving wealth-creating industrial society, and of increasing the collective strength of member states in international negotiations.

This book gives a brief description of Britain's entry into the Community, sets out Britain's general approach to Community affairs and examines British involvement in Community policies.

Further information on developments in the Community are contained in *Current Affairs – A Monthly Survey*, published by HMSO.

[1] The term 'Britain' is used informally in this book to mean the United Kingdom of Great Britain and Northern Ireland; 'Great Britain' comprises England, Scotland and Wales.

Britain and European Union

Background

At the end of the second world war the economies of most European countries were in ruins, their low levels of production leading to adverse trade balances and dependence on North American supplies. At the same time the Soviet Union's influence was expanding, with the establishment of Communist-controlled governments in Central and Eastern Europe. In the face of such economic and political challenges, the countries of Western Europe sought to co-operate in the reconstruction of their economies and to organise themselves in such a way that wars between them would not recur.

Britain and the Scandinavian countries favoured co-operation on an intergovernmental basis, and this view prevailed when, in 1948, the Organisation for European Economic Co-operation (OEEC) was set up to administer the European Recovery Programme (Marshall Aid), aiming to boost European production over a four-year period through the application of United States' aid.

Further steps towards European co-operation were taken in 1949 with the establishment of the Council of Europe, an inter-governmental body created to discuss common political and economic problems. Britain and the other member states are united by a belief in parliamentary democracy.

Formation of the European Community

European Coal and Steel Community

Some countries advocated an early constitutional plan for a federal Europe and the replacement of nation states, while others favoured functional co-operation with new European institutions operating alongside nation states.

As a consequence of the dissatisfaction within European opinion with purely intergovernmental arrangements, a supranational authority in the shape of the European Coal and Steel Community (ECSC) was established in 1952, following the 1951 Treaty of Paris, to embrace the coal and steel resources of Belgium, France, the Federal Republic of Germany, Italy, Luxembourg and the Netherlands ('the Six'). The aim was to establish a common market for coal and steel, to ensure supplies, to promote expansion and modernisation of production and to provide better employment conditions.

Although Britain decided not to participate in the ECSC at that stage, it established a form of association with the new body.

The Rome Treaties

In 1955, having gathered at Messina, Italy, to consider further progress towards European integration, the foreign ministers of the ECSC member states set up an intergovernmental committee to study:

—co-operation over atomic energy;

—the establishment of a common market;

—the creation of a European investment fund; and

—the harmonisation of pay and working conditions.

Although a British representative attended some of the committee's meetings, the British Government had reservations regarding:

—possible overlap with the work of the OEEC;

—the safeguarding of the interests of other countries which, while not associated with these moves towards integration, would be affected by the possible outcome; and

—the supranational approach of the Six.

Consequently, Britain did not take part in the final negotiations leading to the signing on 25 March 1957 of the Treaties of Rome establishing the European Economic Community (EEC) and the European Atomic Energy Community (EURATOM).

Reference to the Treaty of Rome most commonly applies to that establishing the EEC. The Treaty defined its aims as the harmonious development of economic activities; a continuous and balanced economic expansion and an accelerated rise in the standard of living. These objectives were to be achieved by the creation of a common internal market and the progressive harmonisation of member states' economic policies, involving (as detailed in subsequent chapters):

—the elimination of customs duties between member states and of quantitative restrictions on the movement of goods;

—the creation of a common customs tariff and a common commercial policy towards third countries;

—the adoption of common agricultural and transport policies;

—free movement of people, services and capital between member states;

—the elimination of distortions in competition within the common market;

—the approximation of the laws of member states to the extent required for the proper functioning of the common market;

—procedures to co-ordinate the economic policies of member states;

—the creation of a European Social Fund to improve employment opportunities for workers and raise their standard of living;

—the establishment of a European Investment Bank to facilitate economic expansion; and

—the association of overseas developing countries with the Community in order to increase trade and promote economic and social development.

The Treaty provided that the tasks entrusted to the Community should be carried out by the Council of Ministers, the European Commission, the European Parliament and the Court of Justice (see pp 16-23).

The EURATOM Treaty signed in Rome provided for the co-ordinated development of member states' nuclear energy industries and other peaceful nuclear activities (see also p. 91).

Britain and the Six

European Free Trade Association

Britain and six other countries belonging to the OEEC but not to the European Community (Austria, Denmark, Norway, Portugal, Sweden and Switzerland) formed the European Free Trade Association (EFTA) in 1960. The signatories progressively dismantled the barriers to trade between them in industrial goods, but

maintained their own tariffs and their own independent commercial policies towards the rest of the world.

The purpose of EFTA was not only to safeguard and increase
the European trade of its members, but also to provide them with a
base from which to negotiate with the EEC, with a view to
establishing a single European market.

British Applications to Join the Community

Britain had hoped that progressively stronger links could be established between EFTA and the Community. When it became clear
that this would not be possible the British Government began
negotiations, in November 1961, to join the Community.
Denmark, the Irish Republic and Norway also applied for
membership in 1961.

In these negotiations the Government made it clear that it
accepted without qualification the aims of the EEC Rome Treaty.
At the same time, it pointed to the need to negotiate special
arrangements concerning British agriculture and the interests of
Commonwealth and EFTA countries, although it recognised that
these would have to be compatible with the common market.

Since all membership applications required the unanimous
approval of existing Community members, opposition to Britain's
application from the French President, General de Gaulle, led to
the breakdown of negotiations in January 1963. A further application was submitted by Britain in 1967 but, because of the French
Government's continued opposition, it was not possible to reopen
negotiations.

British Accession

When the French political leadership changed in 1969, the
European Commission urged the reopening of negotiations on

Britain's application and those of Denmark, the Irish Republic and Norway. These were resumed in June 1970, shortly after the return to power in Britain of a Conservative Government. The four applicants agreed to accept the Rome Treaties and the decisions taken by the Community since their implementation, and to solve problems of adaptation through transitional measures and not by changes in the existing rules. Throughout the negotiations Britain remained in close touch with its EFTA and Commonwealth partners, especially New Zealand and the sugar-producing countries.

Agreement was eventually reached on the terms of Britain's entry and, in October 1971, both Houses of Parliament voted in favour of membership by substantial majorities. During the debate the then Leader of the Opposition described the terms of entry as inadequate, stating that a future Labour Government would seek a renegotiation.

The Treaty of Accession was signed in Brussels in January 1972 and on 1 January 1973 Britain, Denmark and the Irish Republic became members of the Community, Norway having rejected membership following a referendum.

The Treaty of Accession made arrangements for:

—the progressive abolition of tariffs and the elimination of quotas between the Six and the new member states;

—a progressive adoption of the common customs tariff;

—the adoption of the Common Agricultural Policy with a progressive movement towards Community agricultural support levels;

—provisions on fishing;

—the gradual liberalisation of capital movements;

—an offer of special trading terms to developing Commonwealth countries in Africa, the Caribbean and the Pacific; and

—the continued importation of Commonwealth sugar and New Zealand dairy produce.

The tariff and agricultural pricing arrangements were to be introduced over a five-year transitional period, while those for Britain's contributions to the Community budget (see p. 29), involved a slightly longer period.

Renegotiation of Membership Terms

A Labour Government took office in Britain in 1974 pledged to renegotiate the terms of British membership and to put the issue to the British people in the form of a referendum. Among the new Government's concerns were the system of financing the Community's budget, the costs of the Common Agricultural Policy and the need to improve access to the Community for imports from Commonwealth and developing countries. It agreed to negotiate as far as possible within the provisions of the Treaties and to seek its objectives by securing agreement to changes in the policies and decisions of the Community, provided that Britain's essential interests could be met in this way.

At their meeting in Paris in 1974 the Community's heads of Government agreed to set up a regional fund to correct economic imbalances within the Community.

The first Lomé Convention (see p. 106), signed in 1975, established new trade, aid and co-operation links between the Community and developing countries in Africa, the Caribbean and the Pacific, embodying many of the improvements for which Britain had pressed. Changes were also made to the Community's scheme of trade preferences for developing countries and to its overall development aid policy.

Following the completion of negotiations in Dublin in March 1975, the Labour Government recommended to the British people that Britain should stay in the Community. This recommendation was endorsed by large majorities in both Houses of Parliament. In the referendum held in June 1975, 67.2 per cent of voters supported continued British membership. About two-thirds of the electorate voted.

The European Community

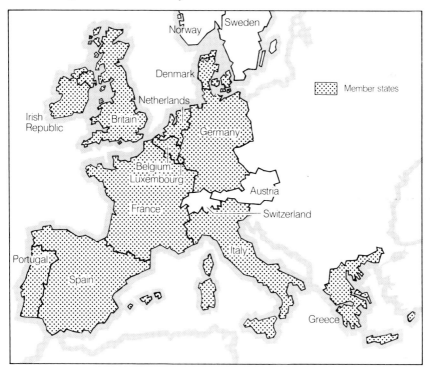

European Union

The signatories of the Treaty of Rome declared themselves 'determined to establish the foundations of an ever closer union between the peoples of Europe'. This aim, to which Britain has been committed since acceding to the Community, has been restated in the Treaty on European Union agreed by Community heads of Government at their meeting at Maastricht in December 1991 and signed on 7 February 1992 (see p. 13).

The nature of European union has never been formally defined. Successive British governments have made clear their opposition to the creation of a unitary state or a federal structure in which national sovereignty would be submerged. In practice, European union has come to signify a step-by-step process of greater co-operation, building on existing policies and elaborating new ones within the framework of the Treaties.

Developments in the 1970s and early 1980s

The years following Britain's accession saw progress in the development of political co-operation machinery, outside the Treaty of Rome framework, to co-ordinate the foreign policies of member states. Progress was also made in the monetary field with the establishment in 1979 of the European Monetary System, envisaged as a first step towards economic and monetary union (see p. 32).

In 1983, at Stuttgart, the European Council issued a declaration on European union. It ranged widely over the objectives of common action, institutional matters and policies, with the emphasis on greater co-operation with respect to foreign policy, cultural co-operation and the approximation of laws. The Stuttgart Council also called for 'broad action to ensure the relaunch of the European Community'.

Britain played a major part in securing the agreement reached at the Fontainebleau European Council meeting in June 1984 on the main issues then dividing the Community—namely, reform of its budgetary arrangements and measures to control expenditure and ensure a fair sharing of the Community's financial burden.

Following this meeting, the Dooge Committee was appointed 'to make suggestions for the improvement of the operation of European co-operation in both the Community field and that of political, or any other co-operation'. In its 1985 report the Committee recommended the creation of a genuine internal market and some institutional reforms, including increased powers for the European Parliament and more effective decision-making in the Council.

Single European Act

Before these matters were considered by the European Council at Milan in June 1985, Britain tabled a proposal for a treaty on political co-operation. Along with other issues, it was submitted to an intergovernmental conference which culminated in the European Council meeting in Luxembourg in December 1985, where agreement was reached on a 'Single European Act'. This came into effect in July 1987, after ratification by all member states, and provided for the following:

1 Completion of the Internal Market—The Community set itself a target date of 1992 for the establishment of a common market in goods and services, and agreed to make greater use of majority voting (see p. 16) on measures designed to complete it. In cases where member states had important interests to protect, decisions would remain subject to unanimity.

2 European Parliament—An amended co-operation procedure was introduced to enable the Parliament to play a more constructive role in decisions on the internal market and in other important areas (see p. 21).

3 Technology and the Environment—The Treaty of Rome was updated to include the collaboration already established in areas of research, technological development and the environment and to provide a basis for future action. In technology, emphasis was placed on market-oriented schemes to improve the competitiveness of European industry.

4 Structural Funds—Co-ordination of the Community's Structural Funds (see p. 60) was improved and the operations of the Regional Fund brought within the Treaty framework.

5 Political Co-operation—Treaty provisions incorporated in the Single European Act formalised and strengthened the commitment to consult and concert action on foreign policy, including the economic and political, but not the defence, aspects of security. These provisions maintained the legal separation between European political co-operation and the European Community.

The British Government welcomed the Single European Act. Commending it to the House of Commons in April 1986, the then Foreign and Commonwealth Secretary stated: 'In a world where no European power can any longer stand on its own, our national goals can be achieved only in co-operation with our Community partners. The most fundamental of these goals has always been the preservation of peace and the enhancement of democracy. The Single European Act serves that fundamental objective. It enhances co-operation in foreign policy, and it enhances our ability to take the steps we need to take as a Community to make ourselves competitive internationally and to create prosperity and jobs.'

Maastricht Treaty

In December 1991 the European Council at Maastricht reached agreement on a Treaty on European Union, comprising changes to the Treaty of Rome and a range of other new Treaty commitments. The Treaty was the result of over a year of negotiation within two parallel intergovernmental conferences on political union and economic and monetary union.

For the Treaty to come into operation, it must be ratified by all 12 member states. In Britain, the ratification process began on 7 May 1992, when the Government published the European Communities (Amendment) Bill, which received its second reading on 20 and 21 May. However, the Government postponed the parliamentary committee stage of the Bill when, on 2 June, voters in Denmark rejected the Treaty by a small majority (50.7 per cent against, 49.3 per cent for) in a national referendum.

While acknowledging the implications of the Danish referendum result, the British Government has maintained its commitment to the Maastricht Treaty and plans to complete the remaining stages of the ratification Bill in 1993. Britain and its Community partners have accepted that the Danish Government needs time to consider its response to the referendum result, but have reaffirmed the importance of concluding the ratification process, without reopening the present text. Member states have agreed that the Community must develop together as Twelve while respecting, as the Treaty does, national identity and diversity.

Provisions of the Treaty

The Treaty creates a European Union, covering the Community's existing and increased responsibilities, and has some new features:

—it embodies the principle of subsidiarity, whereby action should be taken at Community level only if its objectives cannot be sufficiently achieved by the member states acting alone;

—it introduces the concept of Union citizenship, complementing existing national citizenship and conferring new rights for citizens of the Union to vote in elections to the European Parliament and local elections in whichever member state they live;

—it introduces measures of institutional reform, including new powers for the European Parliament (see p. 22), some extension of qualified majority voting in the Council of Ministers (see p. 16) and the establishment of a new advisory Committee of the Regions (see p. 63);

—it strengthens control of the Community's finances, including an increase in the status of the Community's Court of Auditors (see p. 24);

—it provides for the establishment of a common foreign and security policy, conducted on an intergovernmental basis rather than within the existing framework of Community law (see p. 113);

—it endorses a commitment stepping up intergovernmental cooperation on interior and judicial issues, such as asylum and immigration policy and fighting international crime, terrorism and drug trafficking (see p. 98);

—it extends constrained Community competence in certain defined areas of policy relating to regional strategy, transport, telecommunications, energy infrastructures, consumer protection, education and vocational training, environmental objectives and public health; and

—it provides for moves towards economic and monetary union (see p. 33).

The social provisions chapter of the Treaty of Rome remains unchanged and will continue to provide the basis for Community action in social affairs. However, it was agreed at Maastricht that the other 11 member states apart from Britain would pursue additional action in the social field amongst themselves if they so chose (see p. 73).

The Community and its Institutions

Under a treaty signed in 1965, the ECSC, EEC and EURATOM were amalgamated. The Community's institutions are the Council of Ministers, the European Commission, the European Parliament and the European Court of Justice. In addition, the agreement on European Union concluded at Maastricht provided that the Court of Auditors, established in 1977, would henceforth become a Community institution.

The Council of Ministers

The Council of Ministers is the decision-making body on all major legislation and policy and is the only Community institution whose members—usually the foreign ministers or the ministers appropriate to the subject under discussion—represent each country directly in negotiations between member states. The Committee of Permanent Representatives, consisting of member states' ambassadors to the Community, is responsible for preparing the work of the Council and for carrying out tasks that the Council assigns to it. Member states assume the presidency of the Council in rotation every six months. Britain is holding the office again during the second half of 1992.

Voting Procedure

Some questions of policy or principle normally require unanimous agreement in the Council. On other issues the Treaties specify a majority, some articles requiring qualified majority voting, which is a system of weighted voting under which:

—Britain, France, Germany and Italy have ten votes each;

—Spain has eight votes;

—Belgium, Greece, the Netherlands and Portugal have five each;

—Denmark and the Irish Republic have three each; and

—Luxembourg has two votes.

If the Council votes on a European Commission proposal the decision is effective only if there are at least 54 votes in its favour. In some cases voting can take place without the Commission making a proposal, but a decision can then be taken only if 54 votes or more are cast by at least eight member states.

The Single European Act prescribed greater use of qualified majority voting on such issues as the establishment of the internal market. The Maastricht Treaty similarly provides for an extension of majority voting to a limited number of areas. Unanimity is retained for measures where individual states have important interests to protect. Where a member state feels that its vital national interests are involved, it may ask for discussion to continue until an agreement is reached unanimously. Britain believes that this arrangement, introduced in 1966, should remain the basis on which major Community decisions are taken.

Regulations and Directives

The Council has power to make regulations (or Community laws) which are binding on member states and directly applicable. Directives are equally binding as to the aims to be achieved but leave national authorities to decide on the methods of carrying them out. In addition, the Council can issue decisions binding those to whom they are addressed, whether member states, firms or private individuals. Recommendations and opinions are not binding. The Council can also indicate a general policy direction through resolutions.

European Council
Meetings of the European Council are held twice a year by the heads of State or Government (11 prime ministers and the President of France) accompanied by their foreign ministers. The European Commission is represented by its President, who attends on an equal footing with the leaders of the member states.

European Council meetings provide an opportunity for important policy decisions to be taken and for discussions to take place on the development of the Community and world affairs generally.

European Commission
The European Commission is the executive organ of the Community, ensuring that Community rules and the provisions of the Treaties are implemented and observed correctly. It puts forward policy proposals and executes the decisions taken by the Council. It attends all Council meetings, where it participates in discussions as an equal partner.

The Commission administers the Structural Funds established by the Community, prepares a draft budget which must be approved by the Council and the European Parliament and negotiates international agreements on behalf of the Community.

The members of the Commission—two each from Britain, France, Germany, Italy and Spain, and one each from the other seven member states—are nominated by individual governments and appointed with the agreement of all member states. Under the provisions of the Maastricht Treaty, the Commission and its President will be subject to the approval of the European Parliament at the start of their mandate, which will be for five years, rather than the current four-year term, from the beginning of 1995. The Parliament may remove the Commission as a whole from office by a two-thirds majority of votes cast in a vote of censure, though it does not have the power to remove individual Commissioners.

The President of the Commission is responsible for its general administration while each Commissioner is given responsibility for one or more of the main Community activities. The Commission has collective responsibility for all its actions and can take decisions by a simple majority vote.

European Parliament

Membership
The European Parliament, which has 518 members, is directly elected every five years by voters in each member state. The third such election was held in June 1989. Britain, France, Germany and Italy each have 81 seats, while Spain has 60 seats, the Netherlands 25, Belgium, Greece and Portugal 24 each, Denmark 16, the Irish Republic 15 and Luxembourg six. There is no common electoral system for elections to the Parliament.

Of Britain's 81 representatives, 66 are elected in England, eight in Scotland, four in Wales and three in Northern Ireland. British members are elected by a simple majority system in single-member constituencies, with the exception of the members from Northern Ireland, who are elected in one constituency on the single transferable vote system of proportional representation.

Members sit in the Parliament according to party group, of which there are eleven, and not nationality. The 45 British Labour Party members belong to the Socialist group and the 32 Conservative Party members belong to the European People's Party. One of the four remaining British members is a member of the Scottish National Party and sits with the Rainbow group. Of the other three, elected in Northern Ireland, the Democratic Unionist Party member is not affiliated to a group, the Social Democratic and Labour Party member sits with the Socialist group and the Official Unionist member sits with the European People's Party. Each state is responsible for paying the salaries of its representatives, British members having the same salaries and pension rights as members of the House of Commons.

The Parliament meets in Strasbourg on average once a month for sittings lasting five days. Its work is supervised by a Bureau consisting of the President and fourteen Vice-Presidents elected by the members. These are joined by the leaders of the political groups in an enlarged Bureau that organises the agenda for plenary sessions. Officials elected by the Parliament and known as quaestors are responsible mainly for administrative and financial matters and have the right to attend and speak at meetings of the Bureau. When the Parliament is not sitting, committee work takes place in Brussels.

Role and Procedures

Community legislation is enacted by the Council of Ministers, but the Parliament must be consulted about major Community decisions and it has substantial shared power with the Council over the Community budget. Commission proposals are usually submitted to the Parliament by the Council before decisions are taken and it is obligatory for it to submit them in cases stipulated by the Treaty of Rome.

A proposal is first considered by a specialised committee of the Parliament, whose final report is presented for debate during the monthly plenary sessions. Membership of the committees is shared among the political groups in the same proportion as their representation in the Parliament. Officials of the Commission, and sometimes Commissioners, attend the committees to explain proposals. Parliament's opinion, usually in the form of a resolution, is relayed to the Council.

It is usual for the Presidency of the Council to outline the main aims of the Presidency to the whole Parliament and for a minister to inform each committee about Council activities in its area of interest at least once during that Presidency.

Although the British Government considers that the Council of Ministers must be the body that ultimately determines the Community's laws and policies, the Parliament's legislative role was extended by the Single European Act and will be further enhanced by the terms of the Maastricht Treaty (see p. 22).

Under the Single European Act the Parliament can amend a Commission proposal and also, in a second reading, give an opinion on the position adopted by the Council of Ministers on certain categories of legislation, notably that related to the single market. The Commission reconsiders its proposal in the light of the Parliament's amendments. If the Parliament rejects the Council's position, then unanimity by the Council is required for the proposal to come into force as Community law. If the Parliament proposes amendments, the Council votes by qualified majority where the Commission endorses them and unanimously where the Commission has been unable to do so.

Maastricht Treaty Amendments

Under the terms of the Maastricht Treaty, the Parliament could, in certain policy areas, reject by an absolute majority of its members a proposal adopted by the Council of Ministers if agreement could not be reached between the two institutions in a new joint Conciliation Committee. This procedure, applying mainly to Community policies subject to qualified majority voting in the Council, would cover the following areas:

—internal market legislation, including the right of establishment and the free circulation of workers; and

—common policies for research and development, trans-European networks, training, education, culture, health, consumer affairs and the environment programme.

Other Treaty provisions extending the powers of the Parliament stipulate that:

—at the request of a quarter of its members, the Parliament could set up a temporary Committee of Enquiry to investigate alleged contraventions or maladministration in the implementation of Community law;

—an Ombudsman should be appointed by the Parliament to follow up complaints by citizens against Community maladministration;

—in order to strengthen control of the Community's finances, the Parliament would be able to question the Commission on its management of the budget and the Commission would act on the observations of the Parliament;

—Parliament would be able to request the Commission to submit a proposal where it decides by overall majority vote that new Community legislation is needed; and

—the Commission, including its President, would be subject to Parliament's approval at the start of their mandate.

Other Powers
New applications for membership of the Community must receive the assent of an absolute majority of the Parliament, as must the conclusion of agreements with third countries establishing an association involving reciprocal agreements.

The Court of Justice

The European Court of Justice adjudicates on the meaning of the Treaties and on any measures taken by the Council and the Commission. It can, for instance, declare void an act of the Council or the Commission which infringes the Treaties, or whose legality has been challenged by the Council, a member state or an individual directly concerned. In addition, at the request of national courts, the Court gives a preliminary ruling on the interpretation or the validity of Community law. Its rulings must be applied in member states; under the Maastricht Treaty, a member state could be fined for failing to comply with a judgment of the Court.

The Court has 13 judges, including at least one from each member state, assisted by six advocates-general. The latter make reasoned submissions in each case brought before the Court in order to assist it in its interpretation and application of Community law. This is done after the parties have completed their oral and written submissions. The Court is free to accept or reject the advocate-general's conclusions or to reach the same conclusions by a different line of reasoning.

Court of First Instance

The Single European Act included provision for a Court of First Instance to be attached to the Court of Justice. It held its first sittings at the end of 1989. Twelve members sit in the Court, which has jurisdiction over staff cases, certain actions against a Community institution in relation to the Community's competition rules, and certain cases under the ECSC Treaty.

The Court of First Instance has taken over some of the work previously done by the Court of Justice, enabling the latter to consider cases in its own jurisdiction within an acceptable period of time.

The Court of Auditors

Comprising one member from each state, the Court of Auditors:

—audits the Community budget and scrutinises all Community revenue and expenditure;

—advises whether financial management has been sound and reports back to the other Community institutions;

—carries out checks in member states in conjunction with their audit authorities; and

—publishes reports.

The members of the Court of Auditors are appointed by the Council of Ministers for a six-year period.

Consultative Bodies

More than 70 consultative bodies are involved in the Community's work. Among these is the Economic and Social Committee set up under the Treaty of Rome and representing employers, trade unions, consumers and other interests from all the member states. The Commission and the Council of Ministers must consult the Committee on major proposals before decisions are taken, and it is also free to submit opinions on its own initiative.

On matters regarding the coal and steel industries, the Commission and Council of Ministers are assisted by the Consultative Committee representing producers, workers, consumers and dealers. It operates in the same way as the Economic and Social Committee.

Other advisory bodies are concerned with monetary and financial policy, economic policy, social policy, employment, consumer affairs, transport, science and technology, and nuclear research.

The British Parliament and the Community

Ministers representing Britain at the Council of Ministers are accountable to the British Parliament, which is kept informed about the Community and its policies by:

—parliamentary committees;

—regular statements of Council business made by ministers;

—a six-monthly government White Paper on developments in the Community, which is debated; and

—the normal parliamentary question procedure.

Parliamentary Committees

Both Houses of Parliament have select committees which examine proposals for Community legislation and other Community documents. The committees receive draft Commission proposals for legislation which have been submitted to the Council of Ministers.

The British government department concerned also provides an explanatory memorandum describing the subject matter and its implications for Britain.

House of Commons Select Committee on European Legislation

Often referred to as the Scrutiny Committee, it helps Members of Parliament to identify important proposals which might affect matters of principle or policy or involve changes in British law. Government ministers and civil servants may be invited to give evidence to the Committee, and a senior official of the House assists it in dealing with the legal implications of proposals. Further legal advice may be given, where necessary, by the Government's Law Officers.

European Standing Committees

Amendments to the scrutiny procedures were introduced, on a trial basis, from the start of the 1990–91 parliamentary session. Under the new arrangements, documents recommended by the Select Committee on European Legislation for further consideration by the House of Commons are, unless the House otherwise orders, referred to one of two European Standing Committees. Each Committee consists of 13 members nominated for the duration of the session. One deals with matters within the responsibility of the following government departments—Agriculture, Fisheries and Food; Transport; Environment; Forestry Commission (and analogous responsibilities of the Scottish, Welsh and Northern Ireland Offices). The other monitors matters relating to work of other departments.

A Standing Committee may call upon a government minister to make a statement and to answer questions put by members for up to one hour. The Committee may then debate the motion before it for up to two and a half hours (including the time taken by any ministerial statement). The resolution reached by the Committee is then reported to the House; a resolution couched in similar terms is then usually moved in the House without further debate.

House of Lords Select Committee

The terms of reference of the House of Lords Select Committee are widely drawn, for it can identify Community proposals of legal or political importance and report on their merits. The proposals are remitted as necessary to one of several specialist subcommittees, which may call for oral or written evidence from the Government and appropriate outside bodies. The legal implications of Community proposals are examined by a subcommittee chaired by a Law Lord. Reports are made to the House, some of which recommend debate.

Other Means of Information

Every month when Parliament is sitting a report is made by the minister responsible in the Foreign & Commonwealth Office, listing all the Council of Ministers meetings due to be held in the coming month and the subjects expected to be discussed at each meeting. After each Council meeting the minister who attended it reports to the House of Commons, usually in the form of a parliamentary written answer, on the discussions that took place. After meetings of the European Council the Prime Minister reports to the House and is questioned.

Every six months the Government publishes a White Paper summarising developments in the Community and giving an indication of the Government's general approach and policy on specific issues. After its publication the House of Commons holds a wide-ranging debate on Community developments. From the beginning of the 1990–91 session, these debates have been scheduled to take place prior to European Council meetings, in order that they might be more forward-looking.

Members of both Houses may table questions on any Community topic for written or oral answer by the appropriate minister.

Finance and Monetary Policy

The Budget

The Community is financed from revenue contributed by member states, known as 'own resources' and consists of:

—levies collected on trade in agricultural products between the Community and the rest of the world;

—customs duties collected under the common external tariff on imports into the Community;

—value added tax (VAT) levied at a rate of up to 1.4 per cent on a notional harmonised base which is capped at 55 per cent of a member state's gross national product (GNP); and

—a share of the Community's GNP up to an amount required to balance the budget within an own-resources ceiling of 1.2 per cent of GNP (see below).

Over half of the budget covers expenditure on agriculture and 25 per cent covers structural policies (social and regional funds). The remainder covers internal policies, including research and development, and external aid. The Community budget is denominated in European Currency Units (ECUs). The ECU is a composite or basket currency consisting of a specified amount of each Community currency. These amounts, which are based on the economic weights of the member states concerned, were last changed in 1989.

Britain's Contribution
By the end of the 1970s it had become clear that Britain's net contribution was becoming excessive in relation to its share of Community GNP. Accordingly, the British Government sought a correction and, following negotiations, refunds were given to Britain for each of the years in the period from 1980 to 1983.

At the European Council meeting at Fontainebleau in June 1984, the Community agreed on a more permanent arrangement under which Britain received an *ad hoc* lump sum abatement in respect of 1984 and, for later years, an annual abatement of 66 per cent of the difference (in the previous year) between what Britain would have paid to the allocated budget if it had been entirely financed by uncapped VAT and its share of receipts. The Community's VAT ceiling was raised from 1 per cent to 1.4 per cent in January 1986, partly to meet increased expenditure. By the end of 1992, the cumulative value of abatement for Britain totalled over £12,000 million.

Further Budgetary Reforms
Britain attaches great importance to budget discipline and has been a staunch supporter of attempts to control Community expenditure.

New arrangements for Community finances were established in June 1988, in the light of decisions of principle reached by the European Council in Brussels in the previous February. The Council accepted that commitments to the Community's Structural Funds should rise by about £900 million (in constant 1988 prices) a year from 1989 to 1993, which would permit the doubling by 1993 of the resources channelled to less-developed regions within the Community.

It was also agreed that the ceiling on own resources should be expressed in terms of Community GNP rather than VAT. The Community's overall own-resources ceiling for the 12 member states is 1.2 per cent of Community GNP, an increase of about 25 per cent over the previous figure. The cost to other member states of Britain's abatement is outside the ceiling. The own-resources ceiling is currently being reviewed by member states in the light of proposals from the Commission on the future financing of the Community.

The agricultural guideline, an annual ceiling, was also established in 1988. It restricts growth in agricultural market support to no more than 74 per cent of increases in Community GNP.

In order to tighten control of the Community's finances, the Maastricht Treaty provides that, when proposing new measures, the Commission must give assurances that these can be financed within the limits of the EC's own resources. The Treaty also extends the right of the European Parliament to scrutinise the Commission's financial management.

Adoption of the Annual Budget

The Commission is responsible for drawing up a preliminary draft budget based on its own estimates and those submitted by the other Community institutions, and presents it to the Council of Ministers, usually in June. The Council then establishes a draft budget. The Parliament scrutinises the draft and can propose modifications to 'compulsory' expenditure and amendments to 'non-compulsory' items. Compulsory expenditure consists of spending on policies arising directly out of the Treaties, such as the Common Agricultural Policy and expenditure arising from international agreements. All other expenditure—for example staff pay, administration, research and the Regional Development and Social Funds—is non-compulsory. Most new items entered in the budget tend to be classified as non-compulsory.

The Council examines the Parliament's amendments and modifications. If the Council rejects amendments to non-compulsory items, the Parliament can still insist on amendments, within certain limits. It may reject the Parliament's modifications to compulsory expenditure, and the Parliament has no further say in this form of spending. The Parliament's President is responsible for declaring the final adoption of the budget.

The Parliament has the power to reject the budget as a whole if there are important reasons. It has done so twice, in 1979 and 1984. If the budget has not been voted by the beginning of the financial year (1 January), the Treaty of Rome provides for expenditure to be limited each month to one-twelfth of the appropriations for the last adopted budget or one-twelfth of the draft budget, whichever is the lower. The system continues until a new budget is agreed.

European Monetary System

In 1978 the European Council decided to create a European Monetary System (EMS), which came into effect in March 1979. The purpose of the EMS is to establish a greater measure of monetary stability in the Community. It consists of an exchange rate mechanism (ERM), the European Currency Unit and agreed international credit facilities.

Each currency participating in the ERM has an agreed central exchange rate against the ECU, which is used to establish bilateral central exchange rates with the other currencies.

All member states participating in the EMS deposit 20 per cent of their gold and dollar reserves with the European Monetary Co-operation Fund in return for ECUs of the same value. These ECUs may then be used to settle obligations arising from intervention in the foreign exchange markets between the central banks concerned.

Britain, although a member of the EMS since its inception, did not join the ERM until October 1990. Membership was then suspended in September 1992 following a period of worldwide turmoil on the foreign exchange markets.

Economic and Monetary Union

The substantial and important step towards economic integration represented by the adoption and progress of the single-market programme (see p. 38) led to calls by some in the Community for a move towards a single currency and monetary policy. At the request in June 1988 of the European Council, the President of the European Commission produced a report on how such a move could be made.

Britain expressed reservations on the wisdom of a move to a single currency and monetary policy, emphasising the importance of pressing on with the single market. Nevertheless, Britain also made clear its intention to participate fully in the intergovernmental conference that was called by the European Council in June 1990 to discuss amendments to the Treaty of Rome to bring about economic and monetary union (EMU).

Provisions of the Maastricht Treaty
In the negotiations on EMU, the British Government sought to ensure that:

—there would be no commitment by Britain to move to a single monetary policy or to a single currency;

—monetary policy would remain unambiguously a national responsibility until the Community moved to a single currency and monetary policy;

—member states would retain primary responsibility for their own economic policy; and

—the arrangements for EMU would be practical and workable and, in particular, there should be clear and quantifiable convergence conditions which would have to be met by each member state before it could move to a single currency and monetary policy.

The Maastricht Treaty provides for progress towards EMU in three stages: the first, envisaging the completion of the single market, is already underway; the second would begin on 1 January 1994; and the third by 1 January 1999 at the latest, unless the European Council decided earlier that the Community was ready. A special protocol ensures that Britain is not committed to move to the third stage (see p. 36).

In stage two, the European Monetary Institute (EMI) would be established, with a largely advisory and consultative role. As Britain urged, monetary policy would remain under national control. The EMI would continue the work of the Committee of Central Bank Governors and prepare for stage three. Member states would co-ordinate economic policies in the context of agreed, non-binding policy guidelines. The Council of Ministers would be able to investigate member states' budget deficits, on the basis of a Commission investigation and report which would be triggered if a member state breached certain guidelines. The Council could declare deficits 'excessive' if it so decided and issue non-binding recommendations.

By the end of 1996 the European Council would decide whether a majority of member states met the necessary conditions to move to stage three of EMU. If the Council found that enough states did, it could then decide by qualified majority to launch the final stage. If no date had been fixed by the end of 1997, stage three would begin on 1 January 1999.

Reflecting Britain's view that economic convergence is vital before monetary union, member states would have to satisfy the following convergence criteria to participate in this stage:

—average inflation over one year would have to be within 1.5 per cent of the rate of, at most, the three Community countries where it was lowest;

—average long-term interest rates over one year would have to be within two percentage points of the rates prevailing in the above three countries;

—no member state could have a budget deficit which the Council had formally designated as 'excessive'. This would be judged by reference to whether general government net borrowing exceeded 3 per cent of gross domestic product and whether general government gross debt exceeded 60 per cent of GDP, both subject to qualifications; and

—a member state's currency would have to demonstrate successful membership for two years of the narrow band of the ERM, without being devalued.

In addition, account would have to be taken of developments in the Community, such as the integration of markets, member states' balance of payments, unit labour costs and other price indices and the development of the ECU. Member states not meeting the conditions would be given a derogation.

Once the decision to move to the final stage had been taken, a European System of Central Banks (ESCB), consisting of the European Central Bank (ECB) and national central banks, would replace the European Monetary Institute and would be responsible in stage three for monetary policy in the participating member states. In carrying out their tasks and duties under the Treaty, the ECB and the national central banks would be independent. They could not seek nor take instructions from any Community institution, government or other body.

The basic tasks of the European System of Central Banks would be to:

—define and implement monetary policy;

—conduct foreign exchange operations;

—hold and manage official foreign reserves of participating member states; and

—promote the smooth operation of payment systems.

The ECB would have the exclusive right to authorise the issue of ECU banknotes in the participating member states, respecting as far as possible existing practices for both issue and design. Each member state would be able to issue ECU coins subject to the ECB's control on volume, and to the harmonisation necessary for smooth circulation.

In stage three the Council of Ministers would be able to impose sanctions on member states running excessive deficits (although not on Britain if it decided not to move to that stage).

Primary responsibility for economic policy, however, would lie with member states.

Britain's Protocol

British concern that there should be no imposition of a single currency is met by a special protocol to the Treaty recognising that Britain would not be obliged or committed to move to the final stage of EMU without a separate decision to do so by the Government and Parliament.

If Britain decided not to move to stage three, it would retain the pound sterling as its currency, and its own monetary policy. The assumption is that the ERM, or a similar arrangement, would remain in place to provide counter-inflation stability, linking sterling with the single currency and the currencies of any other member states which were not in stage three. Policy making within Britain would remain as it would be in stage two.

Britain would, however, be free to join EMU later if the Council agreed that it met the convergence conditions permitting entry. In common with other member states not participating in stage three, the Bank of England would be represented on a wider body—the General Council of the ESCB—which would continue to carry out co-ordinating and other tasks previously undertaken by the EMI in stage two.

The Single European Market

The programme for completion of the single market—the free movement of goods, people, services and capital—is derived from the European Commission's White Paper, submitted to the European Council at Milan in June 1985. This document outlined a programme to remove the remaining obstacles and distortions in trade between member states by the end of 1992. By the spring of 1992, over 80 per cent of the programme outlined in the White Paper had been agreed.

The Community is Britain's largest export market, with over half of all British exports going there. The Government believes that the single market will benefit the economy of every country in the Community by reducing business costs, stimulating efficiency and encouraging the creation of jobs and wealth. In its view, consumers of goods and services will gain from increased competition that will lead to greater choice and lower prices. The Department of Trade and Industry provides help and advice for businesses on the single market programme.

Movement of Goods

The first ten member states have eliminated duties on internal trade in manufactured goods and most agricultural products, and these will be abolished throughout the Community in 1992 when the transition period following the accession of Spain and Portugal ends. The common customs tariff, which applies to goods from non-member states, will also be extended to these two countries.

Customs duties have already been abolished on most industrial products traded between the Community and members of the European Free Trade Association.

Technical Barriers to Trade

All member states impose a wide range of obligations on business in the interests of safety and consumer protection. Differing requirements and procedures in member states result in technical barriers to trade.

Until the mid-1980s, the Community sought to remove these technical barriers by adopting directives setting out the precise requirements that products had to satisfy before they could be sold freely throughout the Community. This proved a slow process because of the detailed nature of the measures and the difficulty of achieving the unanimity required under the provisions of the Treaty of Rome.

A new approach was introduced in May 1985 to overcome these difficulties. Directives now set out 'essential requirements' (for safety, for example) written in general terms, which must be met before products may be sold in the Community. Technical details are worked out subsequently by the European Committee for Standardisation, the European Committee for Electrotechnical Standardisation and the European Telecommunications Standards Institute. The new approach has been successful in enabling directives to be adopted after a much shorter period of negotiation and covering a broader range of products.

Since 1984 arrangements have been in force requiring member states to notify the Commission in advance of draft proposals for new technical regulations covering industrially manufactured and agricultural products. This gives the Commission and other member states an opportunity to intervene if they consider that the proposed regulation would act as a barrier to trade.

In order to provide an independent check for producers and consumers that a product conforms to a standard or specification, the British Government has encouraged the development of certification schemes, and the accreditation of test laboratories and certification bodies in Britain. The European Organisation for Testing and Certification was set up in 1990 to provide a means of tackling trade barriers arising from different commercial conformity assessment arrangements in the member states.

Reports by the European Commission on standardisation broadly reflect the British view that:

—European standards-making should be more efficient;

—the quality of standards should be maintained;

—standards should be developed to meet market as well as regulatory requirements; and

—international, rather than regional, standards should remain the prime objective.

Physical Barriers to Trade
Another obstacle to trade within the Community is controls on the physical movement of goods across frontiers between member states. This problem has been tackled in a number of ways, building on the elimination of customs duties between Community members.

Britain has supported the Community's moves to reduce customs formalities in order to speed the flow of goods and reduce administrative costs. In January 1988 the Community and the members of the European Free Trade Association introduced a common form for imports and exports, which replaced around 100 different national forms. From 1 January 1993 customs documentation will cease to be required for intra-Community trade.

Regarding the complex question of fiscal frontiers, member states have agreed to apply a minimum standard rate of value added tax from 1 January 1993. The current destination-based system of taxation (taxing of goods in the country of consumption at the rate applicable there) will continue for a transitional period and at least until 1 January 1997.

The British Government has stipulated that any change to an origin-based system must protect Britain's existing zero-rates of VAT on some goods, must be revenue-neutral for individual states and must not impose excessive burdens on business.

Intellectual Property

While the Treaty of Rome prohibits restrictions on imports and exports between member states, these are permitted when they are justified for the protection of patents, designs, trademarks and copyright. The Community is preparing initiatives on patents, trademarks and copyright that will achieve the aims of the single market while continuing to protect intellectual property. Two important directives have been agreed covering the legal protection of semiconductor integrated circuits and of computer programmes.

Movement of People

Freedom to work anywhere in the Community is one of the basic rights laid down by the Treaty of Rome. Nationals of member states can enter another member state to look for work or take a job already arranged. Self-employed people can similarly set up and carry out business. From the end of June 1992 the right of residence in another member state also applies to vocational students, retired persons and anyone who can support themselves without relying on the social assistance system of the host country.

Until recently, professional qualifications gained in one member state were not necessarily recognised in others. A number of directives have now been agreed providing for the mutual recognition of certain qualifications and making it easier for doctors, nurses responsible for general care, dentists, veterinary surgeons, midwives, architects and pharmacists to practise throughout the Community.

In December 1988 agreement was reached on a general system for the mutual recognition of higher educational diplomas awarded on completion of at least three years' professional education and training. The directive, which covers a wide range of professions in Britain and in the rest of the Community, came into force in January 1991. In December 1991 the Council adopted a common position on a second directive extending the system for recognition of qualifications and experience. Britain's National Vocational Qualifications[2] would be recognised under this directive.

The Community aims to make travel between member states easier for people as well as for goods, by relaxing internal frontier controls on Community nationals as far as is compatible with measures to combat terrorism, drug trafficking, crime and illegal immigration, and to safeguard animal and plant health. As a step towards this end, the immigration channels for British citizens and for other Community nationals at points of entry into Britain were merged in March 1989.

[2] A system of accreditation for qualifications awarded for various levels of occupational competence by approved bodies.

Member states began intergovernmental discussions in 1987 on co-ordinating methods of controlling immigration from countries outside the Community. A product of this co-operation has been agreement on a draft convention on crossing external frontiers. This measure would introduce common standards of immigration control at the Community's external frontier, including the use of a shared list of third-country nationals to be refused entry as well as mutual recognition of visas. It would also allow non-EC nationals who are resident in a member state to enjoy visa-free travel for short stays throughout the Community.

Britain and its Community partners have all signed a new European Convention on Asylum, which sets objective criteria for determining which member state is responsible for examining a claim for asylum when more than one member state is involved. In general, it provides that the country which controlled the entry of the asylum seeker into the Community, or the first country in which an asylum claim is made, should be responsible for determining the claim. This would not happen, however, where other factors, such as family reunion or close associations with another country, made it sensible for the claim to be considered elsewhere.

At the European Council in Maastricht in December 1991 it was agreed to bring two aspects of visa policy within Community competence, these being the determination of a list of countries whose nationals will require visas for entry to the Community and a common format for EC visas.

Services

The British Government believes that, as foreseen by the Treaty of Rome, there should be a genuine single market in services as well as goods, on the grounds that existing restrictions increase the costs to European businesses unnecessarily.

Financial Services

Britain attaches importance to the liberalisation of regulations concerning financial services, which account for an estimated 10 per cent of the Community's gross domestic product. At present, providers of financial services from one member state can compete with domestic firms in other member states only if they establish local offices in conformity with national rules and regulations and obtain authorisation from each member state in which a local office is established.

The European Commission's approach to further liberalising measures is based on the mutual recognition of member states' authorities and supervisory bodies, and the setting of minimum safeguards. Directives concerning investment services (under consideration) and the co-ordination of banking (approved in December 1989) will enable banks and investment firms that are authorised to operate in their home member state to operate throughout the Community without the need for further authorisation.

Insurance

A British priority is a real common market in insurance which would be able to compete with the other leading world insurance markets. Community measures already enable insurers in one member state to set up a branch or subsidiary in another to carry on business there on the same terms as domestic insurers in that state.

A second generation of directives was initiated in June 1988 allowing for the provision of insurance across frontiers. The second non-life insurance directive was implemented by July 1990, although under the transitional arrangements full implementation will take place over a longer period in Greece, Portugal and Spain. In November 1990, the Community agreed on a directive designed to apply similar rules to life insurance. This measure is due to be implemented by May 1993.

Agreement on the third life and non-life insurance directives has been reached, providing for insurance companies to operate throughout the Community under a single licence, granted in the member state of the company's head office. The directives are due to come into force on 1 July 1994.

Movement of Capital

The Treaty of Rome envisaged the free movement of capital within the Community as an essential complement to the free movement of goods, people and services. Britain abolished all exchange controls in 1979. A directive removing controls from all capital movements in the Community was adopted in June 1988 and applied to most member states from 1 July 1990. However, Spain, the Irish Republic, Greece and Portugal have until the end of 1992 to comply fully with its terms and, in view of the difficulties posed for countries with less developed financial markets, the last two countries may be permitted a further extension to 1995.

Competition

The Community's competition policy is designed to ensure that trade between member states takes place on the basis of free and fair competition, and that when state barriers to trade are dismantled they are not replaced by private barriers. The policy aims to remove restrictions such as price fixing and market sharing and to ensure that dominant market positions do not adversely affect consumers or other competing firms.

The European Commission administers competition rules and can act on its own initiative, or on complaints from or notifications by member states, companies and individuals.

Merger Control

A regulation which came into force in September 1990 gives the European Commission exclusive jurisdiction over mergers with a Community dimension, meaning those which meet certain turnover thresholds. A merger above the thresholds must be notified to the Commission, which will carry out an investigation of its effects on competition.

State Aids

One of the most important elements in ensuring fair competition across the Community is the Commission's power to oversee, scrutinise and restrict aid given by all member states to their industries. The Treaty of Rome states that any aid which distorts or threatens to distort competition by favouring certain businesses or the production of certain goods is incompatible with the common market. The Commission defines state aids as financial assistance, loans, guarantees and almost any other means of favouring industries and businesses. Some aid is allowed for particular purposes, such as regional or small firm development, but the terms and conditions are carefully determined by the Commission.

The British Government attaches great importance to the application of the state aids rules and continues to support the Commission's efforts to ensure fair competition throughout the Community.

Public Purchasing

Purchasing by governments and other public bodies accounts for as much as 15 per cent of the Community's gross national product. The Commission's programme of legislation is designed to ensure that this aspect of Community trade is conducted in an open and non-discriminatory way.

Two directives on supplies and works subject public bodies to rules on the advertisement and award of contracts above certain thresholds. An additional directive on the provision of services will come into force in July 1993. Suppliers have access to the courts if they feel that there has been a breach of the rules.

A directive governing procurement of supplies and works by utilities in the water, energy, transport and telecommunications sectors comes into effect on 1 January 1993.

Company Law

The Commission's programme for company law is aimed at minimising any difficulties for businesses operating in more than one member state, which might arise from the different legal arrangements in each country. A number of directives have been agreed which harmonise aspects of company law relating, for example, to company accounts and the qualification of auditors. Proposals still under discussion include a draft European Company Statute.

Deregulation

The British Government believes that a liberal business environment is crucial to the successful operation of the single market, which means that regulatory burdens imposed on business, particularly small firms, must be kept to a minimum.

The Commission has been developing a number of proposals to help small firms and improve their understanding of Community programmes and policies. It is also responsible for operating the *fiche d'impact* system, which assesses the cost to business of Commission proposals. Britain is continuing to press the Commission to improve this system by employing it at an earlier stage in the decision-making process and consulting business more widely on ideas for new legislation.

Transport

The Treaty of Rome specifies the establishment of a common transport policy as one of its principal objectives. Although initial progress in implementing such a policy was slow, fresh impetus has been given to it by the Community's move to complete the single market by 1992. It is hoped that by the end of 1992 legislation will be in place providing for liberalisation in all significant parts of transport.

Roads and Road Safety

Although road haulage has expanded since the creation of the Community to the point where industry is often dependent upon it, a number of member states have continued to operate domestic capacity controls and to limit the entry of foreign vehicles. The removal of such restrictions has been a major British objective.

In June 1988 the Council of Ministers agreed to remove by 1993 all quantitative restrictions on the Community's international road haulage market. A temporary scheme to permit the provision of transport services wholly within the boundaries of one member state ('cabotage') by an operator from another member state came into effect in July 1990 and will be replaced by a permanent scheme at the end of 1992. The British Government is pressing for the full liberalisation of international coach services and of road passenger cabotage (within a member state).

The maximum authorised weights and dimensions of commercial road vehicles used in international transport are laid down by Community regulations. Britain, which has lower limits, is exempted from these regulations until the end of 1998.

Progress in harmonising safety and environmental standards for new vehicles has been gaining momentum, covering aspects of design, roadworthiness testing and limits for exhaust emissions. A directive allowing for mutual recognition of driving licences issued by other member states and establishing common standards of health and competence for licence holders will take effect from 1996.

In Britain, responsibility for the major road networks lies with the Government. A Community directive on the assessment of the environmental effects of public and private projects, which came into effect in July 1988, requires assessments to be made for all motorway and major road construction, and for other road schemes where there is likely to be a significant effect on the environment.

In November 1990 the Council of Ministers adopted a three-year *ad hoc* programme for funding transport infrastructure.

Civil Aviation

In June 1992 transport ministers agreed to establish a single market in civil aviation from the beginning of 1993. Airlines meeting harmonised safety and financial fitness criteria will be entitled to an operating licence which will allow virtually unrestricted access to routes within the Community. They will be free to set fares and rates according to their commercial judgment.

Shipping

In December 1986 the Community agreed a common shipping policy to be implemented by 1993 and comprising measures to:

—liberalise the Community's international trade and to ensure freedom to provide shipping services to, from and between member states;

—enable the Community to take concerted action against protectionism by other countries;

—counter unfair pricing practices, particularly state trading lines; and

—establish competition for shipping.

Further development of the common shipping policy, aimed at harmonisation of operating conditions and improving the competitiveness of Community fleets, together with the liberalisation of shipping cabotage, was agreed in June 1992. Britain supports the rigorous application of the Treaty of Rome's provisions on state aids to shipping.

Inland Waterways

Common policies concerning the Community's rivers and canals, which move large amounts of raw materials and industrial goods, focus on reducing over-capacity and barriers to transport.

In late 1991 the Council of Ministers reached agreement on a directive on reciprocal recognition of national boatmasters' certificates and on a regulation to liberalise inland waterway cabotage from 1993.

Railways and the Channel Tunnel

The Community recognises the important role of the railways as part of its transport system and has adopted a number of measures aimed at improving their performance and financial position.

Following the Commission's submission to the Council of Ministers of a Communication on a Community Railway Policy, the Council in December 1989 invited the Commission to set up a working party to consider the development of a high-speed rail network for Europe. The working party's initial recommendations were submitted at the end of 1990.

In June 1991 the Council agreed in principle a directive taking important steps towards liberalisation of access to the European rail network. The directive would allow access by individual rail companies to the railway systems of other member states for the purpose of international combined transport operations and would encourage greater use of rail freight services.

The British Government welcomes improvements in efficiency but believes that railways should be autonomous and manage their business in a commercial way.

In February 1986 Britain and France signed a treaty agreeing to the development, construction and operation of a fixed link across the Channel. The project, which is being undertaken by a privately funded French-British consortium (Eurotunnel), comprises twin single-track rail tunnels (plus a service tunnel) about 50 km (31 miles) long. Eurotunnel will operate a vehicle shuttle for cars, coaches and heavy goods vehicles. The journey time between the two terminals at Cheriton (Folkestone) and Coquelles (Calais) will be about 35 minutes.

In addition, there will be through services operated by British Rail and the French and Belgian railways from London to Paris and

Brussels, taking approximately three hours. Passenger services operating from stations throughout Britain are also planned. Through freight services will run from nine regional terminals in Britain to a network of terminals on the Continent.

Research and Development

Although each Community member state maintains its own national research and development (R & D) effort, no state can on its own meet the challenge of the large markets of Japan and the United States in science and technology. Collaborative research at European level is therefore increasingly important.

Community programmes are designed to improve Europe's technology base and to assist firms in exploiting the internal market. Programmes whose size, scope and resources are approved by ministers, are shared with industry or carried out in the Community's Joint Research Centre, comprising four separate laboratories staffed by scientists from member states.

The British Government actively encourages British companies and organisations to participate in collaborative R & D with European partners in order to maximise economies of scale and to provide access to new technologies and skills which are necessary if British industry is to maintain its competitiveness in European and world markets. British organisations have secured nearly 20 per cent of the funding available under the industrial framework programmes and participate in a large proportion of the projects.

Framework Programmes

Community R & D programmes set out objectives, define priorities and fix overall levels of funding. The 1987–91 framework programme concentrated on industrial technology, covering information technology, telecommunications, biotechnology and manufacturing and materials. Other areas of activity included transport, energy, health, the environment and agriculture. All Community projects focus on pre-competitive collaborative R & D and complement other European programmes such as EUREKA (see p. 59).

The 1990–94 framework programme, involving funding of £5,700 million, was agreed in April 1990. The focus of industrial programmes is on research to develop technology and common standards.

Britain played a major role in defining the technical content and objectives of the individual programmes within the new framework.

Information Technology

The Community's ESPRIT programme—European Strategic Programme for Research and Development in Information Technology—aims to support the development, manufacture and use of information-technology products. Community support is available for up to 50 per cent of project costs. The programme has been implemented in two phases, ESPRIT II (1988–92) building on the progress made in ESPRIT I (1984–88).

A new European information technology programme, to run until 1994, has now been launched. As well as basic research, the programme concentrates on four technical areas—microelectronics, information processing systems and software, advanced business and home computer systems, and computer-integrated manufacturing and engineering.

Telecommunications

In 1987 the Council of Ministers adopted the programme for Research and Development in Advanced Communications

Technologies in Europe (RACE). The aims of the programme are to establish a Community-wide integrated broadband communications system able to transmit all types of telecommunications signals, and to establish a strong Community manufacturing industry in these systems. The development of common standards is a key element of this programme.

Work is carried out by collaboration between industry, academic institutions and telecommunications operators. The Community and participating companies finance projects jointly, usually on an equal basis. Britain is involved in over 70 of some 90 projects under the first phase of the RACE programme, concluding in 1992. A second phase will run until 1994.

Further communications research programmes are under consideration.

Industrial and Materials Technologies

The principal objective of the Industrial and Materials Technology (IMT) programme, running between 1991 and 1994, is to contribute to the rejuvenation of European manufacturing industry by strengthening its scientific and technological base through research and development activities. Industrial companies, universities, other higher education institutions and research organisations are eligible to participate in the programme. Community support is available for up to 50 per cent of project costs. IMT continues the work of the BRITE/EURAM programme, which concludes in 1992.

SPRINT

SPRINT—Strategic Programme for Innovation and Technology Transfer—is a five-year (1989–93) technology transfer programme aimed at improving the competitiveness of small- and medium-sized enterprises. The aim is to ensure that technology and aids to innovation can be shared across national boundaries. Rather than provide support to firms directly, it operates through intermediaries or organisations which help industry to innovate.

Telematics Programme

The 1990–94 Community research programme provides for the funding of projects which will stimulate the development of a trans-European electronic information exchange infrastructure.

The telematics programme, like other Community R & D programmes, is industry-led, requires projects to be collaborative, with partners taken from more than one member state, and is precompetitive. However, it concentrates on the requirements of users of electronic information and their need for inter-operability throughout the EC rather than on the development of new technologies.

The programme looks ahead to the completion of the single European market when the need to transfer information throughout the Community will increase as a result of the deregulatory legislation leading to the free flow of people and goods across the Community. It comprises seven work areas:

—trans-European networks between public administrations;

—transport services;

—health care;

—flexible and distance learning;

—the libraries programme;

—linguistic research and engineering; and

—telematic systems for rural areas.

Natural Resources

Of particular importance within the R & D programme is the management of natural resources. Research activities, directed towards identifying pollution sources and their effects on the environment, contribute to the preparation of quality, safety and technical standards. Research is also undertaken on the prevention of natural and technological hazards. The long-term objective of other parts of the Community programme is to contribute to the development of Europe's potential for understanding and using the properties and structures of living matter.

Energy Programme

The energy programme concentrates on conservation, renewable resources and reduction of adverse effects on the environment, for example the reduction of gases responsible for the greenhouse effect. Research is continuing on:

—nuclear reactor safety, with greater emphasis on radioactive waste management, decommissioning operations and control of fissile materials;

—protection from radiation from natural and medical sources and the furtherance of new technologies to assess quickly the radiological consequences of nuclear accidents; and

—nuclear fusion, specifically the Joint European Torus (JET) project at Culham in Oxfordshire (see p. 90).

Training

An important part of the 1990–94 programme is the training and exchange between member states of research staff in order to pave the way for a genuinely European scientific and technical community. Emphasis is also being placed on training young people embarking on careers in research and technological development. In addition, public and private sector laboratories and research teams are being brought together in collaborative projects.

Other Programmes

Running from 1990 to 1993, the Biotechnology Research for Innovation Development and Growth in Europe (BRIDGE) programme aims to promote the development of modern biotechnology to improve European competitiveness in agriculture and industry. The BIOTECH research programme, covering the period 1992–96, will concentrate on basic biology, with emphasis on the safety assessment of new techniques and novel products.

The Agricultural and Agro-Industrial Research programme forms a part of the Community's programme for 1990–94. It aims to adapt primary production and finished products to the needs of the market and to find new processing methods for raw materials. It also seeks to reinforce the competitiveness of businesses in line with other Community policies, to promote better rural and forestry management and to ensure proper protection for the environment.

The Research Action Programme on materials is designed to increase the Community's level of self-sufficiency in raw materials.

MONITOR, adopted in 1989, aims to identify new directions and priorities for Community research and technological development policy and to help show more clearly the relationship between R & D and other common policies.

The Marine Science and Technology (MAST) programme, the second phase of which runs until 1994, focuses on relevant basic research, including oceanography, coastal engineering, and technologies for the exploration and exploitation of resources.

EUREKA

The 12 member states, together with Austria, Finland, Iceland, Norway, Sweden, Switzerland, Turkey and the European Commission, participate in the EUREKA initiative, designed to improve European performance in the production of high technology goods and services for world markets.

Projects involve co-operation between participants in more than one country in areas such as telecommunications, information technology, robotics, advanced manufacturing, biotechnology and lasers.

EUREKA complements, and is separate from, the Community framework programmes. Projects are concerned more with the exploitation of R & D and are proposed and run by industrial firms and research institutes. Governments supply some funding in appropriate cases and also help by providing information and ensuring open access to markets.

Regional Policy

The Community's Structural Funds, administered by the Commission, are intended to support conversion and development in the Community's less-developed and declining industrial regions. There are three funds: the European Social Fund (ESF), the European Regional Development Fund (ERDF) and the Guidance Section of the European Agricultural Guidance and Guarantee Fund (EAGGF). The ESF supports training and employment measures for long-term unemployed and young people. Infrastructure projects and support for industry, particularly small- and medium-sized enterprises, are financed by the ERDF. The EAGGF Guidance Section supports agricultural restructuring and some rural development measures.

Adopted in June 1988, Community regulations reforming the Funds came into effect in January 1989. These involved a doubling in funding from about £5,700 million (at 1991 prices) in 1987 to £11,400 million in 1993, the bulk of the increase going to the less-developed regions. The reforms have led to a move away from the financing of individual projects towards a strategic multi-annual programme approach.

There are five priority objectives:

—promotion of economic development in the poorest regions;

—converting regions seriously affected by industrial decline;

—combating long-term unemployment;

—facilitating the occupational integration of young people; and

—promoting development in rural areas, as part of the reform of agricultural policy.

The bases for financial assistance from the Funds are the regional plans submitted to the Commission by member states and the Community measures based on them. Decisions on allocation are taken by the Commission in agreement with member states, regional and local authorities and other interested bodies.

European Social Fund

The ESF provides assistance to organisations operating schemes for vocational training and job creation. Public authorities must provide at least as much finance as the Fund. Individual companies can apply to the Fund but they must obtain some funding from a public authority.

The categories of people helped by the Fund include those unemployed for more than 12 months and over the age of 25, those being trained under national vocational education systems, young people leaving school without any training, disabled people seeking jobs and migrant workers requiring training.

In 1991 Britain received over £440 million from the Fund, which helped to support training and employment schemes involving 600,000 people.

European Regional Development Fund

The ERDF is designed to correct regional economic imbalances through projects covering basic industrial infrastructure, transport, telecommunications, and science and research facilities. Support is also given to industry for the building of workshops and the pro-vision of business advice schemes. In some instances the Fund's resources are also directed towards inner city areas in order to restore derelict industrial sites. New productive investment to create jobs lost in declining industries is also financed to a certain extent.

In 1991, commitments to Britain totalled £500 million (provisional), or 10.3 per cent of the Fund's allocation.

EAGGF Guidance Section

The EAGGF Guidance Section finances improvements to roads used for agriculture, the provision of electricity and drinking water for farms, the conservation of rural open spaces, the diversification of agricultural production and the development of forestry.

European Investment Bank

The European Investment Bank provides medium- and long-term loans at attractive interest rates for public and private capital investment projects designed to further the economic development of the Community's less-favoured regions and to improve communications between member states. Types of project assisted include the construction or improvement of roads, railways and rolling stock, airports, ports and ferry terminals; telecommunications; water and sewerage facilities; building of industrial estates; and capital expenditure on institutions of higher education. British projects received nearly 16 per cent of the Bank's lending in 1991.

Each member state subscribes to the Bank's capital, the British share in 1991 being about 19 per cent. The Bank raises the bulk of its funds by borrowing on international and domestic capital markets and lends on a non-profit-making basis. It also provides loans for projects involving small- and medium-sized undertakings; the replacement of oil by other sources of energy; and infrastructure associated with the development of productive activities.

Edward Heath signs the Treaty of Accession to the European Community in Brussels on 22 January 1972.

The Queen speaks to the European Parliament in May 1992.

British Investment in Other Member States

The Marks & Spencer store in Paris.

Aerial view of the Lucas Con-Diesel factory in Barcelona.

The Channel Tunnel

View from inside one of the rail tunnels looking out into the Folkestone Terminal.

Aerial view of Eurotunnel's Folkestone Terminal.

The Royal Shakespeare Company rehearsing *A Comedy of Errors* in preparation for a 1992 British Council tour to Belgium, sponsored by Guinness.

The European Community Youth Orchestra performs a concert in Urbino, Italy, in September 1991.

Community Programmes and Initiatives

Some traditional industries such as steel and shipbuilding have suffered from excess capacity, caused by competition from the newly industrialised countries. As with the Structural Funds, the aim of Community policy is to help create new jobs and promote retraining.

The RESIDER programme, approved in 1988, aims to assist the development of new economic activities in regions affected by the restructuring of the steel industry. It supports improvements in industrial infrastructure and environmental awareness and encourages the growth of small- and medium-sized enterprises through business advisory services, improved access to capital and the promotion of innovation. RESIDER projects are funded jointly by the Community and the member state concerned. Similar schemes, known as the RENAVAL and RECHAR programmes, assist shipbuilding and coalmining areas.

Other Developments

The Treaty on European Union agreed at Maastricht provides for the setting up of a Cohesion Fund before the end of 1993. This would finance projects on environmental protection and transport in the poorest member states.

The Treaty also provides for the establishment of a Committee of the Regions. This Committee, with a four-year term of office and consisting of representatives (nominated by member state governments) of regional and local bodies, would be consulted on matters of major concern to the regions. It would also be able to submit its own opinion on issues involving specific regional interests.

Agriculture and Fisheries

Agriculture

The Community's Common Agricultural Policy (CAP) accounts for over half of the Community's budget. Its stated aims, as set out in the Treaty of Rome, are to:

—increase agricultural productivity;

—ensure a fair standard of living for farmers;

—stabilise the agricultural market;

—guarantee regular supplies of food; and

—provide these supplies at a reasonable price.

Decisions on the level of price support are taken annually by the Council of Ministers on the basis of proposals presented by the European Commission. For many commodities the price support mechanism consists of a minimum intervention price at which agencies of the member states (the Intervention Board executive agency in Britain) will purchase surplus production, and of levies made on imports to maintain internal market prices. Schemes exist for subsidised sales to consumers within the Community, where this can be done without disrupting internal markets. The export of surpluses is made possible by the provision of export refunds to enable Community exporters to sell on world markets at the going price.

Market support arrangements are financed by the guarantee section of the European Agricultural Guidance and Guarantee Fund.

The support prices, as well as rates of export refunds and other aids, are set in European Currency Units and are converted into the currencies of the member states at fixed rates of exchange (commonly called 'green rates'), which do not vary automatically in line with changes in market exchange rates. The green rates can thus be out of line with the market rate of exchange between each currency and the ECU, giving rise to different real support price levels in the different member states.

Monetary compensatory amounts, based on the percentage difference between the green and market rates of each currency, are applied to prevent distortions in trade. They operate as import subsidies and export levies for countries whose currencies' market rates are below the green rates, and as import levies and export subsidies in the opposite case.

The Community is committed to phasing out the differences between green and market rates of exchange by the end of 1992.

Reform

Agricultural production under the CAP has increased considerably in recent years, reflecting rapid technical progress and farming efficiency as well as the high level of price support. As consumption has remained relatively stable, this has resulted in the emergence of surpluses.

Britain has consistently pressed for reform in order to:

—bring demand and supply into better balance;

—increase the role of market forces in agriculture; and

—make environmental considerations an integral part of agricultural policy.

Since 1988 there has been a legally binding limit on CAP market support expenditure and for most commodities there is an automatic cut in CAP support if production exceeds specified quantities.

In July 1991 the European Commission published detailed reform proposals for consideration by member states. Ministerial negotiations culminated in an agreement in principle, reached on 21 May 1992, to reform the CAP in the arable, milk, beef and sheep-meat sectors and on support prices for the 1992–93 marketing year.

The main provisions include:

—a progressive reduction in the support price for cereals from the present level by about 30 per cent from the start of the 1993–94 marketing year. Cereal producers will be offered, in compensation, a direct subsidy on an area basis provided that they agree to take 15 per cent of their arable land out of production;

—a reduction in the intervention price of beef by 15 per cent over three years from 1 July 1993, and the progressive introduction of ceilings from the start of the 1993 calendar year on the annual amount of beef which may be purchased into intervention;

—the freezing of milk support prices for 1992–93, but a cut in the butter support price by 2.5 per cent a year in 1993–94 and 1994–95. Cuts of 1 per cent in national milk production quotas in 1993–94 and 1994–95 have been agreed in principle, subject to review by the Council of Ministers in the light of the market situation at the time; and

—the operation by all member states of programmes to encourage environmentally sensitive farming.

Fisheries

The British fishing industry operates within the Community's Common Fisheries Policy, which provides for the rational conservation and management of fishery resources. Total allowable catches are set each year, their levels based on independent scientific advice, and are then allocated between member states and third countries.

The first six miles of territorial waters are reserved for the member state concerned; there is limited access between six and 12 miles for other member states that have traditionally fished there; and outside 12 miles all members states enjoy access, subject to certain treaty provisions governing Spanish and Portuguese accession to the Community.

The Community's fishing industry is subject to a common market organisation whose primary aims are to:

—encourage the rational marketing of fish products and to implement common marketing standards;

—ensure market stability by adjusting supply to market requirements; and

—guarantee, as far as possible, a fair income to producers (some financial compensation being available in certain circumstances when the market is weak).

The Community operates a common external tariff for fish and fish products, although some preferences are afforded to certain third countries under agreements such as the Lomé Convention (see p. 106), the European Economic Area agreed with EFTA (see p. 102) and bilateral arrangements. Intra-Community trade is tariff-free. Special arrangements apply at present to Spain and Portugal under the terms of their accession to the Community; under these they will not apply the Community's external tariff until 1993 and tariffs which are now levied on some tuna and sardine exports to the rest of the Community are being dismantled.

Fishery relations between the Community and third countries are governed by framework agreements of between two and ten years' duration. Of particular importance to Britain are the recipro-cal agreements with Norway, Sweden and the Faroe Islands, in which each party grants the other's quotas within its waters. There are also 'surplus' agreements, by which the Community pays for access to surplus fish in the waters of a third country. The agree-ment with Greenland is of most importance to Britain.

The Community is also party to a number of international agreements to regulate fisheries on the high seas. The North West Atlantic Fisheries Organisation is the most important of these.

A Community Fisheries Research Programme, funded until 1992, has awarded contracts to projects involving research centres or institutes in two or more member states. The European Commission also makes bursaries available for specific research and is looking at ways of gathering and disseminating information from national research programmes.

Conservation

Fishing activities are also regulated by a number of national and EC technical conservation measures, including limits on the minimum sizes of fish caught, minimum mesh sizes for fishing nets and areas closed to fishing. Each member state is responsible for ensuring that its fishermen abide by the various regulations, and they are monitored in turn by the Community's Inspectorate.

The Council is considering a new package of measures designed to control commercial fishery effort and conserve fish stocks over the period up to 1996. It is proposed that, from 1993, there should be restrictions on the amount of time a vessel can spend at sea, alongside a scheme to decommission fishing vessels. In addition the restrictive licensing system will be extended to all commercial fishing vessels in order to prevent an increase in their number.

Social Affairs

The Treaty of Rome states the need 'to promote working conditions and an improved standard of living for workers', and entrusts the Commission with the task of promoting co-operation among member states in employment, working conditions, vocational training (see p. 95), occupational health and safety, and social security. The Treaty also commits the signatories to the principle that men and women should receive equal pay for equal work, and makes provision for the Social Fund.

Employment

The European Council in June 1989 unanimously agreed three criteria against which all Community action on social and employment issues should be measured. These were that:

—priority should be given to the creation and development of jobs;

—adequate regard should be paid to the principle of subsidiarity; and

—the diversity of practice between member states should be respected.

The British Government believes that the Community has a role to play in supporting action to promote employment, labour flexibility and helping the unemployed back to work. It therefore supports Community efforts to improve training, raise health and safety standards at work and increase labour mobility. It also believes that the Community could have a more prominent role in identifying and disseminating information on effective practice in helping people back to work.

However, the Government is opposed to measures which would, in its view, impose arbitrary restrictions and unnecessary costs upon employers, thereby damaging Community competitiveness in world markets.

Equal Opportunities

The Treaty of Rome states that each member state should apply the principle of equal pay for equal work. In 1975 the Council of Ministers adopted a directive providing for:

—the elimination of sex discrimination regarding pay;

—a right of equal pay for work to which equal value is attributed;

—a right to judicial remedies for workers who consider themselves to be discriminated against; and

—protection against dismissal as a reaction to a complaint or to legal proceedings aimed at enforcing compliance.

A further directive was adopted in 1976 on the implementation of the principle of equal treatment for men and women regarding access to employment, vocational training, promotion and working conditions.

Legislation in Britain makes it unlawful to discriminate on grounds of sex in employment and training, in education and in the provision to the public of goods, facilities and services. It is unlawful for employers to set different compulsory retirement ages for men and women in comparable positions, and it is generally unlawful to discriminate between men's and women's pay if they are doing the same work or work of equal value. Similar legislation on equal pay and sex discrimination applies in Northern Ireland.

A Community directive on equal treatment for men and women in occupational pension and sick pay schemes will become operative at the beginning of 1993. Other directives provide for:

—the application of the principle of equal treatment for self-employed men and women and protection of self-employed women during pregnancy and motherhood; and

—the gradual implementation of the principle of equal treatment for men and women in statutory social security schemes.

Health and Safety at Work

The first health and safety measures were taken under the Treaty of Paris in the coal industry, concentrating on mine safety and elimination of dust associated with respiratory diseases.

In 1978 the Council of Ministers adopted a programme providing for the exchange of knowledge, harmonised action against dangerous substances, limitations on noise levels in work places, and the drawing up of schemes providing information on safety to particular groups of workers. The Community has since approved a series of measures providing for:

—the preparation of safety assessments and emergency plans for certain hazardous industrial activities; and

—the protection of workers from the risks associated with exposure to lead, asbestos, biological agents, carcinogens and noise.

Harmonisation of health and safety legislation is a central feature of the 'social dimension' of the single market. The single market programme envisages the implementation of some 40 health and safety proposals.

In 1989 the Council of Ministers approved a framework directive, to be implemented by the end of 1992, under which employers will be required to assess risks and introduce necessary preventive measures. The directive also makes provision for training on health and safety and for the consultation of workers or their representatives on health and safety matters.

Other directives have been adopted covering workplace safety, use of work equipment and personal protective equipment, and the health and safety of temporary workers.

Under the Single European Act a series of directives is emerging on product safety, covering technical standards and safety requirements for specific products.

The period from 1 March 1992 to 28 February 1993 was designated by the Community as the European Year of Safety, Hygiene and Health at Work.

Information and Consultation Rights for Workers

The Commission has drafted a number of proposals which would impose statutory requirements on employers to inform and consult their employees, and provide for worker participation in decision-making. Several member states operate statutory participatory systems which reflect the traditions and practices of their systems of industrial relations. The Commission has proposed a European Company Statute which would impose obligations on employers in respect of worker information, consultation and participation.

The British Government is opposed to binding Community legislation in the field of employee involvement. It believes that in Britain such arrangements should be agreed voluntarily between employers and employees. The benefit of the voluntary approach is the flexibility it allows for employers to develop schemes which are best suited to their own business needs and circumstances and the needs of their employees.

Social Charter and Social Action Programme

The Community Charter of Fundamental Social Rights of Workers, or Social Charter, arose out of the European Commission's desire to add a social dimension to the single market. The Charter covers a wide-ranging series of matters connected with employment, such as pay, working hours, leave, social benefits, vocational training, equal opportunities, worker consultation and participation, and measures for the disabled and elderly.

The Charter was endorsed by 11 of the 12 member states at the European Council's meeting in Strasbourg in December 1989. The British Government opposed the Charter on the grounds that it did not take into account differences in national practice and that it failed to address the overriding concerns of job creation and competitiveness. It also believed that many of the areas covered in the Charter should be decided at national rather than Community level.

The Social Charter, as a political declaration, had no legally binding effect. The Commission therefore introduced its Social Action Programme to give practical effect to the principles contained in the Charter. The programme comprised some 47 proposals for Community action, about half of which were for binding legislation. By May 1992, 38 of these proposals had been published, of which 21 had been agreed or adopted by the Council or Commission.

The Treaty on European Union agreed at the Maastricht European Council confirmed that the social provisions chapter of the Treaty of Rome would remain in force and unamended. A separate social protocol was also agreed which noted that the 11 member states other than Britain wanted to pursue the objectives of the Social Charter and that they had drawn up an agreement among themselves to do so. The protocol would allow the 11 member states to take common action going beyond the provisions of the Treaty of Rome. Britain would not take part in any such negotiations, and any measures that were adopted would not be applicable to Britain.

Poverty

Between 1975 and 1980 an initial Community programme of pilot schemes and studies to combat poverty took place. A further programme was established for the period 1985 to 1989, focusing on such groups as the unemployed, the elderly, single-parent families and second-generation migrants. Funding was provided for research and public-awareness campaigns, practical projects aimed at improving understanding of the nature, causes and extent of poverty, and methods of exchanging ideas among member states.

A third programme, running from 1989 to 1994 with a budget of £36 million, provides for pilot projects and innovatory measures aimed at integrating the economically and socially less privileged groups in society. The Community normally contributes half of the estimated costs of agreed projects. The remainder is provided by local or national agencies, or by voluntary or private organisations in the countries concerned.

Social Security

As part of Community efforts to promote the free movement of labour, regulations provide for equality of treatment and the protection of certain social security rights, including health care, for employed people going to another member state. They also cover retirement pensioners and other beneficiaries who have been employed, as well as their dependants.

Under the regulations a person's social security contributions in one country can often count towards a benefit or pension claimed in another, contributions usually being paid under the social security legislation of the member state in which the person is employed.

Cash benefits include family allowances and those for sickness and maternity, retirement, invalidity, accidents at work and occupational diseases, and unemployment. A person covered by the regulations is also entitled to receive urgent medical and dental treatment when visiting another member state on the same terms as insured nationals of that state. Community nationals who are not covered by the regulations but who have entitlement to medical treatment under a social security scheme are also entitled to receive urgent medical treatment when on a visit to another member state. As a consequence of an initiative from Britain, the Community's social security regulations also apply to self-employed people.

Health

The Community's second 'Europe against Cancer' programme, for 1990–94, was adopted in May 1990. The aim of the plan is to improve understanding of the causes of cancer and its prevention and treatment. It includes provision for projects related to:

—prevention and screening;

—public information and health education;

—professional training; and

—co-ordination of research.

In June 1991 a decision on an action plan for 1991–93 under the AIDS (acquired immune deficiency syndrome) programme was adopted by the Council of Ministers. The plan involves exchanges of information and expertise and examples of good practice.

The Community's principal programme for health research is the Biomedical and Health Research Programme, which is running between 1990 and 1994 and concentrates on the following areas:

—prevention, care and health systems;

—major health problems and diseases; and

—biomedical ethics.

Health research also features in other Community programmes such as BIOTECH (see p. 58) and the Telematics Programme (see p. 56).

The Maastricht Treaty would give the Community competence to encourage co-operation between member states in the area of the prevention of diseases by promoting research into their causes and transmission, as well as health information and education.

There is a continuing programme of research and exchange of information on drug demand reduction within the Community. The Commission produces an annual report on demand reduction programmes in member states. The first European Drug Prevention Week took place in November 1992 during Britain's presidency, involving national and Community-wide events. The European Council has agreed that a European Drugs Monitoring Centre should be established. Health Ministers considered the problem of the use of drugs in sport in December 1990 and June 1991. A Code of Conduct on Doping in Sport was adopted in January 1992 and has been widely disseminated.

Standardised health warnings on tobacco products are effective from 1992 under a directive on labelling adopted in 1989. A further labelling directive, adopted by the Council of Ministers in May 1992, requires additional health warnings on non-cigarette tobacco products from January 1993. A directive to reduce progressively the tar yield of cigarettes was adopted in 1990. No decision has been made on a proposed directive to ban the advertising of tobacco.

Negotiations are continuing on Commission proposals for harmonising member states' licensing decisions on medicinal products and for creating a European Medicines Evaluation Agency.

The Environment

Environmental pollution does not respect national boundaries and European co-operation is essential to conserve nature and protect wildlife. The Community's environmental objectives, as set out in the Single European Act, are to:

—preserve, protect and improve the quality of the environment;

—contribute towards protecting human health; and

—ensure a prudent and rational utilisation of natural resources.

Most Community environmental directives, regulations and decisions are concerned with such issues as water and air pollution, the disposal of wastes, noise, and the protection of wildlife.

A European Environment Agency has been proposed in order to bring together environmental information from existing bodies for the use of member states and the Commission and to ensure comparability of data throughout the Community.

In March 1989 the Community signed the United Nations Basle Convention on the Control of Transboundary Movement of Hazardous Wastes and their Disposal.

Air Pollution

Three directives were adopted in the early 1980s setting mandatory air-quality standards and monitoring requirements for sulphur dioxide and particulates, lead, and nitrogen dioxide. In 1984 an air pollution framework directive was agreed as a first step in the harmonisation of national legislation on the control of industrial air pollution.

In 1988 the Community agreed a directive to reduce emissions from power stations and other large combustion plants. Under its terms, emissions of sulphur dioxide—which contributes to acid deposition—from existing plants must be 60 per cent lower than 1980 levels by 2003. Emissions of nitrogen oxides will have to be reduced by 30 per cent by 1998 using the same 1980 baseline. In order to meet these reduction targets, the British electricity supply industry is investing in a major programme of capital expenditure, including for example the fitting of flue gas desulphurisation equipment, and specialised (low-NOx) burners to some power stations.

Two directives setting combustion conditions and emission limits for municipal waste incinerators took effect from December 1990. The European Commission is preparing a hazardous waste incineration directive, which Britain supports, in the interests of protection of public health and the environment.

A new directive requiring the monitoring and reporting (to the Commission and, above certain levels, to the public) of ground level ozone, which is a noxious air pollutant, has been adopted by the Council of Ministers.

Global Warming and Ozone Depletion

In October 1990 Britain agreed with its EC partners to take action aimed at stabilising total emissions of carbon dioxide (the main greenhouse gas) at the 1990 level by the year 2000 in the Community as a whole. This objective assumed that other leading countries take similar action.

Britain has subsequently played a leading role in the negotiations towards the United Nations framework convention on climate change. This will commit developed countries which ratify it to adopt policies and measures aimed at returning emissions of carbon dioxide and other greenhouse gases to their 1990 levels by 2000.

The Commission set out a proposed strategy in October 1991 for meeting the Community objective, based on a combination of:

—national strategies;

—Community programmes on, for example, energy efficiency and renewable energy; and

—a Community-wide energy tax.

In May 1992 the Commission issued further proposals for an energy tax, the adoption of which would require unanimity among member states. The Commission proposes that adoption of a tax should be conditional on the EC's major competitors taking similar action to limit emissions, a view supported by the British Government.

Britain has sent a report on its national programme to limit carbon dioxide emissions to the Commission, as all member states were requested to do by the Council of Ministers in December 1991.

Britain and its EC partners are closely involved in international efforts to control chlorofluorocarbon gases (CFCs) and other ozone-depleting substances, which are used as aerosol propellants, refrigerants, in foam-blowing and as solvents. Britain and the Community were among the initial 25 signatories of the 1987 Montreal Protocol on Substances that Deplete the Ozone Layer. The Protocol provided for the production and consumption of CFCs to be reduced by 50 per cent of 1986 levels by 1998–99. It also froze the consumption of halons—ozone depleting substances used in fire fighting—at 1986 levels from 1993.

The Protocol was strengthened in June 1990 when signatories agreed to phase out CFCs, halons and carbon tetrachloride by the year 2000. There were provisions for exemptions for any agreed essential uses of halons. It was also agreed that methyl chloroform would be phased out by 2005.

The Community agreed in December 1990 to a faster phase-out of the production and consumption of CFCs, other than for essential purposes, by mid-1997.

The Montreal Protocol is to be revised again in November 1992. Preliminary discussions, co-chaired by Britain, began in April. Britain has urged a stricter timetable for phasing out CFCs and the other controlled substances and, in March 1992, the Community agreed to propose that they should be phased out by the end of 1995.

Water Pollution

Arrangements for technical co-operation and exchange of information have been established between the Commission and the governments of Austria, Canada, Japan, Sweden, Switzerland and the United States, and some research has been undertaken with other Western European countries. A Community information system assists member states faced with a spillage of oil or other harmful substances at sea.

The Community has signed:

—the Paris Convention on the Prevention of Marine Pollution from Land Based Sources;

—the Barcelona Convention for the Prevention of Marine Pollution in the Mediterranean;

—the Bonn agreement for co-operation in dealing with pollution of the North Sea by oil and other harmful substances; and

—the Convention for the Protection of the Rhine against Chemical Pollution.

A series of conferences on the North Sea, attended by eight states with North Sea coasts (including Britain) and the European Commission, provide the prime focus for British policy towards the marine environment. Measures adopted are applied in all Britain's coastal waters including the Irish Sea.

As a result of a British initiative at the 1987 North Sea conference a task force, comprising senior marine scientists and administrators from the eight coastal states and the Commission, was set up to make a detailed assessment of the environmental health of the North Sea. A quality status report is due to be published in 1993. The next full North Sea conference will be held in 1995.

In December 1990 the Council of Ministers agreed a regulation establishing a programme of action for the protection of the Mediterranean Sea. This programme provides funds to help deal with the serious environmental problems affecting the Mediterranean. A similar financial programme for measures to help protect the Community's northern coastal waters has also been agreed.

The Community has adopted a directive on the quality of bathing waters which specifies a standard of cleanliness, including bacteriological criteria. Britain is currently engaged in a £2,000 million programme to bring all its designated bathing waters up to standard—76 per cent of its identified bathing waters passed the standard in 1991 compared with 66 per cent in 1988.

A directive adopted in May 1991 requires the provision of proper sewage treatment facilities for all substantial population centres. These are required to be in place from 1998 to 2005 according to size and location of discharge. Britain took a lead in pressing for agreement on this directive, and incorporated many of its objectives into British practice before the directive was adopted—notably planning the phasing out of sewage sludge dumping at sea, and the introduction of treatment for all significant discharges of sewage effluent to coastal and estuarial waters.

Agreement was reached in June 1991 on a directive to protect underground and surface water from nitrate pollution from agricultural sources. The directive requires member states to designate 'vulnerable zones' where the concentration of nitrate in water exceeds specified levels, or where environmental problems are occurring. Within vulnerable zones member states must take action to limit the application of chemical fertiliser and manure and introduce measures to reduce nitrate leaching. Two years are allowed to designate known vulnerable zones, a further two years to establish action programmes, and four more years to implement such programmes. The directive was formally adopted in December 1991.

Drinking Water

A directive setting Community standards for the quality of drinking water was approved in 1989. Regulations setting drinking water quality standards in England and Wales, which were adopted in 1989, incorporate, and in some respects go further than, the requirements of the EC directive. The water supply industry in England and Wales is carrying out improvement programmes designed to bring virtually all drinking water up to standard by 1995.

Vehicle Emissions

Emissions from motor vehicles are also controlled through Community directives. Following a British initiative, the Council of Ministers adopted a directive in 1985 requiring unleaded petrol to be generally available throughout the Community by October 1989. In Britain, a substantial tax differential has been created in favour of unleaded petrol, the market share of which has risen to over 40 per cent. Under a Community directive agreed in 1987, all new cars registered in Britain since 1 October 1990 have to be capable of running on unleaded petrol.

In June 1991 the Council of Ministers adopted an amending directive setting stricter emissions limits for cars and light vans from the beginning of 1993. This involves the fitting to nearly all new petrol-engined cars of three-way catalytic converters, designed to convert carbon monoxide, hydrocarbons and nitrogen oxides to carbon dioxide, water and nitrogen.

A directive tightening emission standards from diesel-engined heavy goods vehicles was adopted in October 1991. New controls will come into effect in 1992, 1993, 1995 and 1996.

Other Measures

In the early 1980s the Community adopted the so-called 'Seveso' directive in order to minimise the human and environmental risks from chemical accidents. The directive is undergoing a fundamental review in order to strengthen environmental protection.

In December 1991 the Council of Ministers formally adopted a directive on hazardous waste to replace an existing directive on toxic and dangerous waste dating from 1978. The directive provides for the clear definition of hazardous waste and controls its mixing and movement. The regulation concerning exports and imports of certain dangerous chemicals was amended, enabling importing countries to decide whether or not to allow the import of an internationally agreed list of dangerous chemicals.

A common position has been adopted by the Council of Ministers on a regulation which provides for the collection and evaluation of data on existing chemical substances and, if necessary, proposals for controls. In addition, the Council has approved a directive on the classification, packaging and labelling of damaging substances and the notification of new chemical substances. Britain also takes part in the chemicals programme of the Organisation for Economic Co-operation and Development which, in co-ordination with the Community, provides for the collection and evaluation of data and reduction of risk from harmful chemical substances.

Pressure from Britain has been instrumental in securing the introduction of a Community scheme for labelling environmentally less harmful products. The scheme, which will be voluntary and excludes food and drink, will inform consumers, encourage the development of less environmentally damaging products and facilitate trade. Work is in hand to define the criteria for the award of the label for some 10–12 product groups, with a view to the scheme being launched in late 1992. Primary responsibility for awarding labels will rest with individual member states, although there will be safeguards to ensure criteria are uniformly applied across the Community.

The Commission published a proposal in March 1992 for a Community scheme of voluntary environmental audits, called 'Eco-audits'. Under the proposal, which would initially apply to industrial sites, businesses would be able to pursue environmental programmes and management systems and gain Community-wide recognition for their efforts. Britain is sponsoring, jointly with the Commission, the development of codes of practice for the independent verification of Eco-audits. During the British presidency of the Community, political agreement on the Eco-audit proposal by the Council of Ministers will be a priority issue.

A regulation establishing a new Community fund for the environment (LIFE) was agreed in December 1991, bringing together several existing funds and incorporating a number of new areas for Community support. Projects which could benefit from Community assistance include nature protection measures, development of clean technologies, efforts to protect the marine environment, and environmental education, training and information initiatives.

Britain's partners have responded favourably to its proposal for a Community environment inspectorate to ensure that enforcement agencies within the member states apply EC legislation effectively and consistently.

Wildlife

Reflecting its concern for the protection of wildlife, the Community acceded to the Berne Convention on the Conservation of European Wildlife and Natural Habitats in 1982 and to the Bonn Convention on the Conservation of Migratory Species of Wild Animals in 1983. Both conventions have been ratified by Britain.

The Community applies the Convention on International Trade in Endangered Species. Conservation measures promoted by Britain have included a ban on the import of whale products and harp and hooded seal-pup skins, and stricter controls for the protection of wild birds. In February 1992 the Commission proposed a major revision and extension of these measures.

In November 1991 the Council of Ministers adopted a regulation on the importation of certain furs and the use of leghold traps, which will be banned throughout the Community by January 1995. There will be a ban from that date on the importation into the

Community of furs of certain animals from countries which have not prohibited the use of the trap or which do not use traps that meet internationally agreed standards.

After several years of discussion, the Council of Ministers agreed a directive in December 1991 to protect habitats and wild flora and fauna, in accordance with the Berne Convention. The directive will establish a network of special areas of conservation, known as Natura 2000, for rare, endangered and vulnerable species and habitats across the Community.

Other Common Policies

Energy

The high price of energy in the 1970s and early 1980s focused attention on the Community's dependence upon imported oil for over half its energy supplies. The Gulf crisis of 1990–91 further emphasised the vulnerability of the supply and price of oil. The Community objectives set in 1987 were to:

—keep oil consumption to about 40 per cent of total energy consumption;

—improve energy efficiency by at least 20 per cent;

—continue the role of natural gas in energy supply; and

—increase output from renewable energy sources.

The Community is working towards the establishment of a real internal energy market. As a first step towards this objective, the Council of Ministers has adopted directives on the liberalisation of transfrontier trade in gas and electricity supplies and on price transparency. Commission proposals for further liberalisation are under consideration by the Council.

European Energy Charter

The European Energy Charter was signed in 1991 by the Community and its member states, together with other member countries of the Organisation for Economic Co-operation and Development, other European countries and the republics of the former Soviet Union. The Charter seeks to promote:

—trade in energy in line with major multilateral agreements, through open and competitive markets, access to energy resources and exploration and development on a commercial basis, and other means;

—co-ordination of energy policies and mutual access to technical and economic data; and

—energy efficiency and environmental protection, including the use of new and renewable sources of energy and clean technologies.

The Charter contains provisions on the role of commercial enterprises. Investment protection and open competitive energy markets are promoted in order to encourage such enterprises to make the investments needed, particularly in Eastern Europe and the republics of the former Soviet Union. It is also expected that the Charter, by bringing energy prices to market levels, together with the transfer of modern technology, will increase efficiency and reduce waste and pollution.

Other Community Initiatives

The Community recognises the harmful effects that energy production and utilisation have on the environment. It has agreed to stabilise carbon dioxide emissions at the 1990 level by the year 2000 in the Community as a whole (see p. 79).

Under its SAVE (Specific Actions for Vigorous Energy Efficiency) programme, adopted by the Council in October 1991, the Community intends to bring forward energy-efficient measures in the light of current environmental and energy security concerns.

Through SAVE, the Community is working towards agreement on a common energy labelling scheme for electrical appliances and minimum efficiency standards for household electrical equipment, such as fridges and washing machines, and for industrial heating. Agreement on energy efficiency standards for new hot water boilers has already been reached.

The European fusion programme's main project is the Joint European Torus (JET) at Culham in Oxfordshire, which was set up to demonstrate the scientific feasibility of nuclear fusion. A proposal to extend its operations until 1996 has been approved by the Community.

The Community's non-nuclear research and development programme covers solar energy, biofuels, wind energy and geothermal energy. Long-term research into the last has involved the pooling of member states' resources.

In 1990 the Community introduced the THERMIE scheme for the promotion of energy technology, including support for demonstration projects in the oil and gas sector. Commission proposals for the establishment of competitive non-discriminatory licensing systems for oil and gas resources have been submitted to the Council of Ministers.

British Energy Policy

Britain, with the largest energy resources of any Community country, is actively engaged in international collaboration on energy questions. Britain's energy policy is designed to ensure the secure, adequate and economic provision of energy to meet its needs.

The Government seeks to ensure that all economic forms of energy are produced, supplied and used as efficiently as possible and, where feasible, through competitive energy markets. It promotes the continued profitable development of Britain's oil and gas resources, the development of a competitive coal industry, the safe and economic development of nuclear power, and the most cost-effective use of energy through the adoption of energy efficiency measures. It also funds an extensive research and development programme into renewable sources of energy.

Britain regards energy efficiency as the cornerstone of any sustainable energy policy in Europe and throughout the world.

The Government's Energy Efficiency Office provides a wide range of services and programmes designed to encourage cost-effective energy efficiency improvements, including:

—the promotion of combined heat and power schemes;

—the Home Energy Efficiency Scheme, which provides grants for draughtproofing and insulation to low-income households; and

—the Energy Management Assistance Scheme, which helps smaller enterprises to improve their energy efficiency.

European Atomic Energy Community

In 1957 the original six member states signed the Treaty setting up the European Atomic Energy Community (EURATOM), with the task of:

—promoting and co-ordinating nuclear research for peaceful purposes in member states and a Community programme of research and training;

—disseminating technical information;

—establishing and applying uniform health and safety standards;

—facilitating capital investment; and

—introducing arrangements to prevent nuclear materials from being diverted from their intended uses.

Other matters covered by the Treaty concern the creation of a common market in specialised material and equipment, the free movement of capital, and freedom for nuclear specialists to work within the Community. The Commission is responsible for the Community research programme, part of which is being conducted in its Joint Research Centre, and also co-ordinates work within the integrated nuclear fusion programme.

Under the EURATOM Treaty, the provisions of which are legally binding on all member states, the Commission is empowered to exercise control over certain specified nuclear materials. Other provisions stipulate that operators must supply the Commission with details about the basic technical characteristics of their installations and that they should maintain records accounting for ores, source materials and special fissile materials. The Commission may impose sanctions in the event of any infringement of the provisions. In Britain, the Government ensures that these obligations are fulfilled.

Other International Agencies

Britain and all the Community member states are members of the 23-nation International Energy Agency. Since its establishment in 1974, the Agency has adopted a wide range of co-operative measures to reduce member nations' dependence on imported oil and to share oil stocks in the event of emergency. It continues to support the adoption of realistic energy pricing policies by all member countries, as well as encouraging measures to stimulate the efficient use of energy and the diversification of energy supplies of member states.

Britain is also a member of the International Atomic Energy Agency, which is responsible for international activities regarding the peaceful uses of nuclear energy. The Agency encourages research, fosters the exchange of scientific and technical information and provides a focus for work on international standards for nuclear safety and radiation protection. It also administers nuclear safeguards designed to ensure that fissionable and other materials are not diverted illegally to further any military purpose.

Consumer Protection

Since 1975 the Community has been developing a programme of consumer protection and information based on five rights: protection of health and safety, protection of economic interests, redress, access to information and education, and the right to appropriate consultation and representation.

Community directives are in place to control misleading advertising, to protect consumers against defective products and to establish essential safety requirements which all toys must meet. A Community-wide collection of home and leisure accident statistics involving products helps to identify areas where common protective action is needed. In October 1991 the Council reached agreement on a common position over manufacturers' liability to their customers for the safety of their products.

The British Government believes that the interests of consumers are best served by a combination of national and Community action.

Education and Training

Individual member states of the Community are responsible for the content of teaching courses and for the organisation of their education systems, although there is co-operation on vocational training and freedom of movement. The Maastricht Treaty on European Union respects this provision, but endorses Community action aimed at:

—developing a European perspective to education;

—encouraging mobility of students and teachers and co-operation between educational establishments; and

—developing exchanges of information.

ERASMUS

In 1987 the Council of Ministers adopted the European Community Action Scheme for the Mobility of University Students (ERASMUS), under which grants are provided to enable Community students to study in other member states. Some 102,000 students have benefited from the scheme to date.

The scheme also promotes an inter-university student exchange programme whereby students spend a period of study in another member state as part of their course. The third element of the programme concerns the improvement of academic recognition of diplomas and periods of study.

Since the introduction of the scheme, about 180 British higher education institutions have participated in it and, as a result, some 19,000 British students have been able to spend a period of study abroad. A second phase of the ERASMUS programme is running until 1995.

LINGUA

The EC's LINGUA programme is designed to encourage the teaching and learning of foreign languages throughout the Community. It gives grants towards joint educational projects and exchanges for young people (aged 16 to 25) undergoing professional, vocational and technical education. It also covers in-service teacher training for foreign language teachers, programmes of co-operation for in-service training institutions and measures to develop language training materials for business. The programme, agreed by the Council of Ministers in 1989, runs until the end of 1994.

Vocational Training

The Council of Ministers has adopted measures to promote the vocational training of young people and adults, particularly in response to technological advances. The European Centre for the Development of Vocational Training in Berlin assists the Commission in providing information about new training methods.

The Community Action Programme in Education and Training for Technology (COMETT) aims to foster co-operation between higher education and commercial enterprises in technological training. Its activities include:

—setting up consortia of universities and enterprises to analyse the training needs of companies;

—organising student placements in companies in other member states;

—arranging fellowships to enable personnel from industry to go on secondment to institutions of higher education; and

—funding the development of courses in technology.

Initiated in 1987, the programme's second phase will run until 1994.

The EUROTECHNET programme promotes vocational training for new technology, operating through a Community-wide network of demonstration projects which disseminate good training practice.

The Community's FORCE programme, running from January 1991 to the end of 1994, encourages continual vocational training of workers in EC companies through transnational partnership projects and exchange visits between trainers and training specialists. Out of 170 innovatory projects financed throughout the Community in 1991, 23 were led by British promoters. The PETRA programme promotes training exchanges for young people within the Community.

Other Community initiatives seek to ensure that the qualifications of one member state can be recognised in another (see p. 42).

TEMPUS

The Trans-European Mobility Scheme for University Students (TEMPUS) began in 1990. The purpose of the scheme is to:

—support the development of the higher education systems of the countries of Central and Eastern Europe; and

—encourage their interaction and co-operation with partners in the European Community through joint activities and mobility.

European Schools

Community member states have created nine European schools in order to provide a multinational education for the children of staff employed in Community institutions. They are day schools for pupils aged between 4 and 19. A common curriculum is followed leading to the European Baccalaureate, the schools' own leaving examination which is recognised throughout the Community for entry to universities and other institutions of higher education.

One school at Culham in Oxfordshire serves families working at the Joint European Torus project and at the European Community offices in London. The other eight schools are situated in Belgium, Germany, Italy and the Netherlands.

Other Institutes

The Commission supports numerous research institutes on European affairs and European documentation centres in universities and other higher education establishments. Britain has over 40 documentation centres and a number of European depository libraries, all of which receive Community documents and publications.

The European University Institute in Florence organises postgraduate study programmes on European issues and their historical, political, economic and legal aspects. It contributes to the understanding of European culture and science and studies the development of European countries and institutions in relation to each other and other parts of the world.

Culture

Community involvement in cultural affairs has been limited, partly because of a desire to avoid duplicating the cultural work of other organisations—for example, the Council of Europe. Community action has focused largely on business aspects, such as the free movement of cultural goods and services, improving living and working conditions for artists and performers, and creating new jobs through the promotion of tourism and regional creativity.

In 1985 the Community adopted the annual event of the European City of Culture, starting in Athens. The subsequent Cities of Culture have been Florence, Amsterdam, Berlin, Paris,

Glasgow, Dublin and, in 1992, Madrid. Community funds have been made available for conservation work on monuments of Community-wide importance or buildings in underdeveloped regions whose restoration would bring economic benefits. The Community has also helped to create the European Community Youth Orchestra, which is regarded as one of the finest in the world.

More recently, the Council of Ministers has agreed to encourage links between non-governmental cultural organisations. Also, the Commission has been invited to examine the extent to which archives policy and practice within the Community should be co-ordinated.

The British Council's 'Britain in Europe' project, running from October 1989 to the end of 1992, is designed to promote British arts and culture in the Community. Sponsors are invited to invest in major arts events, thereby providing British companies with promotional opportunites for their activities in the Community.

Terrorism and Crime

Because of the threat posed by international and other terrorism, member states have sought to act jointly against it. They have agreed not to export arms or other military equipment to countries clearly implicated in supporting terrorist activity, and to take steps to prevent such material being diverted for terrorist purposes.

It is European Community policy that:

—no concessions should be made under duress to terrorists or their sponsors;

—there should be solidarity between member states in their efforts to prevent terrorism and to bring the guilty to justice; and

—terrorist attacks against any member state should be met with a concerted response.

Community internal affairs and justice ministers meet frequently to discuss common measures directed against terrorists, drug traffickers and other criminals. The British Government believes that, with the introduction of the single market at the end of 1992, some frontier controls will need to be retained to ensure that such people do not enjoy unlimited freedom to move from one member state to another.

In December 1991 the European Council agreed to set up a central European Police Office (EUROPOL) to help combat drug trafficking and other serious forms of organised crime.

The Community attaches great importance to anti-drugs co-operation, which focuses on law enforcement, international co-operation, assistance to developing countries, education and health. A committee co-ordinates Community anti-drugs work and a European political co-operation working group deals with the international aspects. Britain and its Community partners believe that the problem of drug misuse requires a comprehensive strategy designed to tackle demand and supply. They fully support the work of the United Nations in combating drug trafficking and they also participate in regular meetings of the Council of Europe's Pompidou Group dealing with anti-drugs measures.

The Community and its member states have endorsed Britain's proposal for a European Drugs Intelligence Unit which will now form part of EUROPOL.

External Economic Relations

Under the Treaty of Rome the Community, which is the world's largest trading unit, is pledged to promote world trade, development and peace.

Most countries have diplomatic representatives accredited to the Community, which has its own delegations to the United States, Canada, Japan and countries in Latin America, Africa, Asia, the Caribbean and the Pacific, the Organisation for Economic Co-operation and Development and the international organisations based in Geneva. The Community has observer status at the United Nations.

In international trade negotiations the Commission negotiates on behalf of the Community as a whole, under a mandate from the Council of Ministers.

Commercial Policy

The Treaty of Rome pledges the signatories to contribute to the harmonious development of world trade, the progressive abolition of restrictions on international trade and the lowering of customs barriers. It also provides for a common commercial policy, which includes tariff rates, export policy, measures to liberalise trade and action against unfair trade, such as the elimination of tariff barriers or action against dumping or subsidies.

General Agreement on Tariffs and Trade
Acting on behalf of the Community, the Commission takes part in bilateral and multilateral trade negotiations, the latter being

conducted mainly within the framework of the General Agreement on Tariffs and Trade (GATT).

The GATT has been in existence since 1947 and aims to reduce and remove barriers to trade. There are over 100 signatories to the Agreement and some 30 other countries apply it on a provisional basis. There have been seven previous rounds of GATT negotiations and the eighth round, known as the Uruguay Round, has been in progress since 1986. Its main concerns are to:

—bring trade in agriculture and textiles fully within the GATT system;

—strengthen the GATT system so that it can deal more effectively with trade distortions and disputes;

—achieve further reductions in tariff and non-tariff barriers; and

—extend GATT disciplines to the new areas of intellectual property, investment and services.

The Uruguay Round was due to be completed in December 1990; however, a number of difficult issues, particularly agriculture, still remain to be resolved and the negotiations are continuing.

Britain is committed to the open multilateral trading system and the principles of GATT. It wants to see all countries taking on a greater share of GATT obligations, according to their level of development, and supports further market opening and reduction of trade barriers in both developed and developing countries.

Multi-Fibre Arrangement

The Multi-Fibre Arrangement (MFA), introduced in 1974, consists of a series of agreements covering international trade in textiles and clothing and is designed to balance the interests of developed importing nations and developing exporting countries.

Under the Arrangement, the Community has bilateral agreements with 27 low-cost supplying countries. These agreements either limit by quota the import into the Community of textiles and clothing, or provide for the introduction of quotas if imports threaten the Community's textile industry. Other suppliers are covered by similar arrangements. The present MFA was to expire in July 1991 but has been extended to the end of 1992, pending its phasing out as part of the Uruguay Round.

Economic Agreements

In addition to the arrangements under the Lomé Convention, the Community has concluded preferential agreements with Mediterranean countries and non-preferential co-operation agreements with a number of countries and groups of countries in Asia and Latin America.

European Free Trade Association
The seven EFTA countries (Austria, Finland, Iceland, Liechtenstein, Norway, Sweden and Switzerland) together form the Community's largest trading partner.

The Community and EFTA have agreed to create a European Economic Area (EEA), which will come into effect at the beginning of 1993 and which will extend Community provisions on the free movement of goods, services and capital to the EFTA countries. The EEA will comprise a market of over 375 million people, accounting for some 40 per cent of world trade, and will facilitate accession to the Community for those EFTA countries which wish it.

The main features of the agreement include:

—free movement of Community and EFTA products within the EEA;

—the liberalisation of trade in financial services, transport, telecommunications and audio visual services;

—the adoption by EFTA of competition and state-aid rules based on those of the Community;

—mutual recognition of professional qualifications; and

—increased co-operation on the environment, research and development, consumer protection and social policy on the basis of Community actions.

The negotiated agreement is a success for Britain and others who want to see a market-oriented Community which is outward looking and open to new members.

The United States

The Community has close economic ties with the United States, its second-largest trading partner. In 1991 exports to the United States amounted to $86,481 million, and imports from the United States to $103,208 million. There are also important links through investment.

In November 1990 the Community and the United States reached agreement on a declaration emphasising the importance of strengthening their partnership. It set out common goals including:

—support for democracy;

—respect for human rights and individual liberty throughout the world;

—the maintenance of peace and security by fostering international co-operation; and

—the development of a sound world economy based on market principles and an open multilateral trading system.

There are twice-yearly meetings between the Presidents of both the European Council and the European Commission on the one side and the President of the United States on the other.

The Mediterranean and the Middle East

The Community has concluded individual co-operation or association agreements with virtually all non-member countries with a Mediterranean coastline, plus Jordan. Their terms vary in detail, but all provide duty-free access to Community markets for most industrial goods and varying degrees of preferential access for agricultural products. The Community also provides development aid.

An economic co-operation agreement is in force with the six member states of the Gulf Co-operation Council—Bahrain, Kuwait, Oman, Qatar, Saudi Arabia and the United Arab Emirates. It provides for co-operation in agriculture and fisheries, industry, energy, science and technology, investment, the environment, training and trade. Negotiations are in progress which may lead to the establishment of a free trade area embracing the Community and the Council.

Latin America

Britain supports the establishment of closer links between the Community and Latin America. In December 1990 member states of the Community and the Rio Group—Argentina, Bolivia, Brazil, Chile, Colombia, Ecuador, Mexico, Paraguay, Peru, Uruguay and Venezuela—agreed to conduct annual ministerial meetings and regular consultations on matters of common interest. Similar arrangements apply to the relations between the Community and the Central American states.

The Community has concluded many trade and economic co-operation agreements with individual Latin American countries or regional bodies, covering economic, industrial, scientific and technical matters, trade promotion and co-operation on energy. It is also supporting moves towards regional integration in Latin America and promoting training.

Almost all the Community's exports to Latin America are manufactured goods, while over 50 per cent of Community imports from the region consist of agricultural produce and foodstuffs. Energy, ores and metals comprise a third of the Community's imports.

The Community and its member states are Latin America's second largest source of official development assistance, which is concentrated on the least developed countries in the region. It covers rural development, food aid, emergency relief aid, economic co-operation and support for regional integration.

China and Japan

A wide-ranging economic co-operation agreement between the Community and the People's Republic of China has been in force since 1985. Sanctions adopted by the Community against China in 1989 following the repression of political opposition by the Chinese Government were relaxed in October 1990.

Japan is the Community's third-largest trading partner in terms of the value of visible bilateral trade. Although the market in Japan for manufactured and other products is essentially open, the Community is continuing to press for the full liberalisation of sectors where restrictions remain, in order to encourage imports and thereby help to reduce Japan's current account surplus in its trade with the Community.

In July 1991, the Community and Japan adopted a joint declaration affirming their intention to consult each other on major issues and, whenever appropriate, to co-ordinate their positions.

They also agreed to strengthen their co-operation and exchange of information. Under the agreement there are annual meetings between the Presidents of the European Council and of the Commission on the one side and the Japanese Prime Minister on the other.

Motivated in part by the development of the single market, a number of Japanese companies have sited manufacturing plants in the Community—for example, the Nissan car manufacturing plant in the north-east of England. Britain has attracted about 40 per cent of Japanese direct investment in the Community, far more than any other member state.

In July 1991 agreement was reached on a transitional arrangement for imports of Japanese motor cars into the Community after 1992. The arrangement will apply until the end of 1999, after which trade will be completely free.

Developing Countries

The European Community and its member states are among the main sources of official aid to developing countries. Although the bulk of this aid is provided bilaterally by member states, the Community has an important role, its main instrument being the Lomé Convention. This is an aid and trade agreement with 69 countries in Africa, the Caribbean and the Pacific—the ACP states. About half of the Community's aid is supplied under the Convention. The Community provides aid to developing countries in Asia and Latin America, food aid and humanitarian help.

The Lomé Convention

The first Lomé Convention was signed by the Community and 46 ACP states in 1975. Co-operation between them has since been strengthened and extended under successive conventions, the fourth of which entered into force in September 1991. This latest agreement between the Community and 69 ACP states will expire in 2000.

The Convention provides the ACP countries with duty-free and quota-free access to the Community for all their industrial products (except rum) and most agricultural products. As a result of special arrangements secured at the time of Britain's accession, it contains special provisions for sugar, bananas and beef, reflecting the importance of these products for several Commonwealth countries among the ACP group. Countries producing cane sugar are granted indefinite access to the Community market for nearly 1.3 million tonnes annually at guaranteed prices.

Community aid is provided from the European Development Fund (EDF) and loans are available from the European Investment Bank (EIB). During the first five years of Lomé IV, £7,700 million will be available from the EDF and up to £850 million from the EIB. Britain's contribution to the EDF will be about £1,300 million. These financial arrangements will be reviewed after five years.

The Convention provides for increased consultation between the Community and each ACP state to ensure that aid is put to the best possible use within the context of the recipient country's own policies. Emphasis is placed on:

—agriculture and food production;

—raising rural incomes and standards of living;

—developing local processing of agricultural produce;

—ensuring a better balance between food and export crops; and

—encouraging agricultural research.

The Convention also contains measures to combat drought and desertification and to increase the contribution of the fishing industry to food supply. Aid is available to help ACP states finance imports for regional projects and for emergencies.

Lomé provides the ACP countries with compensation for shortfalls in their export earnings from certain agricultural commodities, including cocoa, coffee, cotton, copra and ground nuts. This is known as the STABEX system. There is also a special loan fund, known as SYSMIN, which provides loans at low interest rates to finance projects to increase the export capacity of mineral producers whose production and income have suffered as a result of disruptions beyond their control.

Humanitarian Aid and Emergency Relief
During 1991 the Community responded to appeals for humanitarian aid from 40 countries in Asia, Africa, Central and Eastern Europe and Latin America, providing money and basic necessities such as food, shelter and medical provisions. Humanitarian aid in 1991 totalled about £560 million, representing 21 per cent of the Community's total development aid. The remaining development aid budget is targeted for long-term development.

Humanitarian aid is provided both by individual member states and by the Community, acting through international agencies and non-governmental organisations. A Development Council resolution in 1991 provides for an exchange of information between member states and the Commission and for co-ordination of humanitarian aid.

The food-aid component of humanitarian aid, on which the Community spent some £310 million in 1991, includes food for distribution in emergency situations and food for free distribution to vulnerable groups such as the elderly, children and refugees. The Community usually pays the additional costs of food-aid transportation. In addition, at least 40,000 tonnes of cereal are sent annually to the World Food Programme's International Emergency Food Reserve.

All Community emergency aid is given on a non-reimbursable basis and made available as soon as possible. Medicine and medical equipment, personnel, food and finance for essential repairs are usually sent in the aftermath of a disaster.

Community spending on emergency operations in 1990 and 1991 was four times greater than the 1986–89 total of £140 million, the Horn of Africa and the Middle East absorbing almost 80 per cent of the 1991 total.

Community humanitarian aid is also given to refugees and displaced persons. For the victims of the Gulf crisis (see also p. 115), the Community and member states provided 40 per cent of the $1,900 million global emergency aid response for the Kuwaiti, Iraqi and Kurdish refugees.

Generalised System of Preferences

The European Community's Generalised System of Preferences (GSP) scheme, first introduced in 1971, is designed to increase the export earnings of developing countries, promote their industrialisation and accelerate their rate of economic growth.

The scheme provides duty-free access to the Community for industrial and textile products from developing countries, and preferential entry for a limited range of agricultural products (mainly processed), often at reduced rates. Almost all industrial products are granted duty-free access, but there are some restrictions in the case of very competitive products from the most advanced developing countries. The poorest countries are exempted from such restrictions and are granted special treatment for agricultural products.

Non-Associated States

The Community's aid programme for the developing countries in Asia and Latin America not covered by the Lomé Convention or having any other special relationship with the Community will be worth some £1,925 million for the period between 1991 and 1995. Priority is given to rural development and agricultural production in the poorest countries, most of which are in Asia, and economic co-operation with the better-off countries.

A non-preferential co-operation agreement has been in force since 1980 between the Community and the Association of South East Asian Nations (ASEAN—Brunei, Indonesia, Malaysia, the Philippines, Singapore and Thailand) providing for commercial and economic co-operation. It is designed to encourage collaboration in science and technology, energy, transport and communications, agriculture and fisheries. The signatories have also undertaken to extend to each other arrangements for investment promotion and protection. A special section of the agreement is devoted to development co-operation. Joint ASEAN-Community investment committees have been established in the capitals of the ASEAN states. Britain welcomes and supports close links between the two groups.

Eastern Europe and the Former Soviet Union

The Community has taken steps to enhance its relations with the emerging democracies of Central and Eastern Europe and to consolidate reform and economic development. Since 1988, the Community has signed trade, commercial and economic co-operation agreements with Albania, Bulgaria, Czechoslovakia, Hungary, Poland, Romania and the Baltic states of Lithuania, Latvia and Estonia.

Following Britain's advocacy of association agreements with the fastest reforming countries, the Community began negotiations in December 1990 with Czechoslovakia, Hungary and Poland. Agreements concluded in December 1991 envisage the establishment of a free-trade area within ten years and provide for political dialogue at ministerial and official level. They also contain provisions for lending from the European Investment Bank and for co-operation in a wide range of sectors. By offering Czechoslovakia, Hungary and Poland significant trade advantages, the agreements are designed to encourage economic development and so help these countries towards realising their aspirations to eventual Community membership. Negotiations on similar association agreements are under way with Bulgaria and Romania.

Under the Group of 24 (G24)[3] umbrella, the Community contributes to balance of payments support loans to the countries of Central and Eastern Europe. The Community has also committed some £885 million under the PHARE programme of technical assistance for economic restructuring in Poland, Hungary, Czechoslovakia, Bulgaria, Romania, Albania, the Baltic states and Slovenia.

In addition the Community has provided substantial food aid and humanitarian assistance to Central and Eastern European countries, most recently to Albania and the Baltic states.

The Community's TEMPUS student mobility scheme (see p. 96) began in 1990.

European Bank for Reconstruction and Development
At the end of 1989 the European Council agreed to create a European Bank for Reconstruction and Development aimed at

[3]The Group of 24 comprises European Community and EFTA member states, the United States, Japan, Canada, Australia, New Zealand and Turkey.

promoting private enterprise in Central and Eastern Europe. Shareholding countries and international organisations—including Britain, the European Community and the European Investment Bank—signed an agreement in May 1990 establishing the Bank. The agreement entered into force in March 1991 and the inaugural meeting of the members of the Bank, which is sited in London, was held the following month. Other members include countries to which the Bank lends, plus the United States, Japan and Canada.

Community member states, the Community itself and the EIB together have a majority holding in the Bank. Britain holds 8.5 per cent of the shares.

The Former Soviet Union
In December 1990 the Community approved the provision of food aid and a credit guarantee for food purchases (totalling about £525 million) for the former Soviet Union, in order to support the process of economic and political reform that was then being pursued. A further £875 million loan for food and medical products and £595 million in technical assistance were subsequently agreed by the Community.

In view of the critical food situation in Russia, the European Council agreed in December 1991 to another food-aid grant of £140 million to help principally the populations in Moscow and St Petersburg.

European Political Co-operation

The Single European Act (see p. 11) committed Community member states to the process of political co-operation under which they formulate and implement agreed positions on major international issues. The agreement reached at the Maastricht European Council on the establishment of a common foreign and security policy builds on the effectiveness of this existing mechanism, and has been fully endorsed by the British Government.

Britain has taken a leading role in the development of European political co-operation and the Community's voice has become increasingly influential on the world stage.

Common Foreign and Security Policy

The Maastricht Treaty provides for the establishment of a common foreign and security policy which 'shall include all questions related to the security of the European Union, including the eventual framing of a common defence policy, which might in time lead to a common defence'.

The policy would be implemented through intergovernmental procedures in the Council of Ministers, although the Commission would be associated with the work carried out and the European Parliament would be kept regularly informed. It would be outside Community competence and the jurisdiction of the European Court of Justice.

The Council of Ministers would decide, on the basis of general guidelines from the European Council, that a matter should be the subject of joint action, setting out the scope and objectives of such action and the means and procedures for its implementation. All significant decisions would continue to require unanimity in the Council. Whenever there was any plan to adopt a national position, or to take national action pursuant to a joint action, the Council would be informed accordingly to allow for prior consultations.

Concerning representation at the United Nations, the Treaty provides that Community member states which were also members of the UN Security Council would 'concert and keep other member states fully informed'. Those member states which were permanent members of the Security Council (Britain and France) would, 'in the execution of their functions, ensure the defence of the positions and the interests of the Union, without prejudice to their responsibilities under the provisions of the United Nations Charter'.

Defence

The Maastricht agreement states that:

—the policy of the Union should not prejudice national defence policies and should respect NATO obligations;

—the Western European Union (WEU)[4] would be developed as the defence component of the European Union and as the means to strengthen the European pillar of the Atlantic Alliance and to formulate a common European defence policy;

—the operational role of the WEU would be strengthened;

—those Community countries not currently in the WEU would be invited to join, while other European states could become associate members;

—the new Treaty defence provisions would be revised by 1998 on the basis of a report to be presented to the European Council in 1996.

[4]The WEU comprises Belgium, Britain, France, Germany, Italy, Luxembourg, the Netherlands, Portugal and Spain.

The Middle East

Arab-Israeli Dispute

Community policy towards the Arab-Israeli dispute has been guided by the European Council's Venice Declaration of 1980, requiring the acceptance of two basic principles—the right of all countries in the area, including Israel, to a secure existence within guaranteed borders, and the right of the Palestinian people to self-determination.

Member states have repeatedly called upon Israel to withdraw from territory occupied in 1967, and, in the meantime, to administer its occupation in accordance with international law and human rights standards. On Britain's initiative, the Community granted to Palestinian producers preferential trade access to EC markets on the same terms as those agreed with Israel. The Community also provides aid to Palestinians, both directly and through the United Nations Relief and Works Agency.

The Twelve have given full support to the Middle East dialogue, involving bilateral and multilateral negotiations between Israel and the Arab states, which were inaugurated in October 1991, under the co-sponsorship of the United States and the former Soviet Union. Community member states have reiterated their commitment to play a constructive and active role in the multilateral talks.

The Gulf Conflict

The Community strongly condemned Iraq's invasion of Kuwait in August 1990, reinforcing the consensus among all members of the United Nations Security Council and the international community as a whole on the need to restore international legality. Member states complied strictly with the UN sanctions regime imposed on Iraq, insisting that Iraq withdraw its forces unconditionally and restore Kuwaiti sovereignty.

Iraq's refusal to comply with UN Security Council resolutions led to military intervention in early 1991 by the UN-sponsored international coalition. Iraqi troops were expelled from Kuwait after a brief campaign in which United States' and British forces took the most active role. The Community has fully endorsed subsequent UN efforts to eradicate Iraq's weapons of mass destruction, as well as measures to protect Kurdish refugees fleeing violent repression by the Iraqi regime.

The Former Soviet Union

The abortive coup in the Soviet Union in August 1991 heralded the disintegration of the Communist structure and the independence of the constituent republics.

At the end of August 1991 Community member states agreed to establish diplomatic relations with the Baltic states of Lithuania, Latvia and Estonia, the Soviet takeover of which in 1940 has never been accepted by Britain and many other countries. At the end of 1991 the Soviet Union ceased to exist and was replaced by the new Commonwealth of Independent States (CIS) which comprises the other former republics.

Britain and its Community partners welcomed the Russian Government's acceptance of the former Soviet Union's international commitments and responsibilities. They also said that they would recognise the other former republics in the Commonwealth once they had received certain assurances. The Community required that new states in Eastern Europe and in the former Soviet Union would have to:

—respect the provisions of the UN Charter and the commitments in the Helsinki Final Act and the 1990 Charter of Paris on the rule of law, democracy and human rights;

—guarantee the rights of minorities and ethnic and national groups;

—respect the inviolability of all frontiers, which could be changed only by peaceful means and common agreement;

—accept all commitments on disarmament and nuclear non-proliferation and on regional stability and security; and

—commit themselves to settle by agreement all questions concerning state succession and regional disputes.

Having obtained the necessary assurances, the Community has since extended recognition to all the former Soviet republics as independent countries. The Community has contributed substantial sums to help sustain the political, economic and social stability of the newly independent states, and to encourage democratic reforms, the introduction of market economies and regional co-operation.

Former Yugoslavia

Britain and the other Community member states have striven to bring an end to fighting in former Yugoslavia, which followed declarations of independence by Slovenia and Croatia in June 1991. Fighting took place in Croatia between Serb and Croatian forces.

In an effort to secure a lasting ceasefire, the Community convened a peace conference from September 1991 chaired by Lord Carrington, a former British Foreign and Commonwealth Secretary. It also provided a monitor mission. Community member states also supported the establishment in 1992 of a United Nations protection force set up to monitor a ceasefire between Serbia and Croatia.

In December 1991 Britain and its Community partners agreed to recognise Yugoslav republics meeting the same conditions as former Soviet republics (see p. 116). In January 1992 Slovenia and Croatia were consequently given recognition, as was Bosnia-Hercegovina in April.

After Bosnia's independence, fighting broke out between Serbs, Croats and Muslims living in the territory. Efforts were made by the Community and Lord Carrington to bring this fighting to an end. A ceasefire was agreed but soon broke down. At the end of May 1992 the Community imposed United Nations economic sanctions on Serbia because of its failure to take effective measures to cease its interference in the fighting in Bosnia.

In August 1992 the Community and the United Nations organised a peace conference in London where various commitments were made by the parties to the dispute. It was agreed that joint mediation would in future be undertaken by the Community and the UN.

Southern Africa

The Community has consistently encouraged moves to abolish the system of apartheid in South Africa and to create a genuine national dialogue on the country's future. Major changes announced since February 1990 have met many of the Twelve's demands—notably the release of Mr Nelson Mandela and other political prisoners, the lifting of the ban on the African National Congress and other organisations and the repeal of apartheid legislation.

To encourage more reforms and to help prevent the process being undermined by economic recession, the Twelve have relaxed progressively the restrictive measures imposed on the South African Government, most recently lifting the 1985 ban on crude oil exports in April 1992. This followed the endorsement by white South Africans in a referendum in March 1992 of the process of constitutional negotiation, initiated in December 1991, for transition to a non-racial, democratic state.

There is a voluntary code of conduct for Community companies with subsidiaries in South Africa, which is designed to improve conditions for black employees, including their freedom to join trade unions, and to remove racial discrimination at work.

The Twelve supported the implementation of the United Nations plan for Namibian independence, which began in April 1989, and made their own contributions to the UN Transitional Assistance Group set up to monitor the holding of elections to a constituent assembly. Member states welcomed Namibia's achievement of independence in March 1990 and its decision to sign the Lomé Convention.

Addresses

Ministry of Agriculture, Fisheries and Food, 3 Whitehall Place, London SW1A 2HH.

Ministry of Defence, Main Building, Whitehall, London SW1A 2HB.

Commission of the European Communities, Jean Monnet House, 8 Storey's Gate, London SW1P 3AT

Department for Education, Sanctuary Buildings, Great Smith Street, London SW1P 3BT.

Department of Employment, Caxton House, Tothill Street, London SW1H 9NF.

Department of the Environment, 2 Marsham Street, London SW1P 3EB.

Foreign & Commonwealth Office, King Charles Street, London SW1A 2AH.

Department of Health, Richmond House, 79 Whitehall, London SW1A 2NS.

Home Office, 50 Queen Anne's Gate, London SW1H 9AT

Overseas Development Administration, 94 Victoria Street, London SW1E 5JL.

Department of Social Security, Richmond House, 79 Whitehall, London SW1A 2NS.

Department of Trade and Industry, Ashdown House, 123 Victoria Street, London SW1E 6RB.

Department of Transport, 2 Marsham Street, London SW1P 3EB

HM Treasury, Parliament Street, London SW1P 3AG.

Further Reading

Community legislation and other documents are published in the *Official Journal*. Other Community publications include the *Bulletin of the European Communities*, which is published 10 times a year, and the European Commission's annual report. The European Parliament issues a brief account of each session, the full texts of debates being published in the *Official Journal*. Community publications are issued in various languages by the Office for Official Publications of the European Communities (L-2985, Luxembourg), its British agents being Her Majesty's Stationery Office. A wide range of information about the Community is available from the London information office of the European Commission.

Official Publications

			£
Developments in the European Community (published every six months).	HMSO		
Treaties Establishing the European Communities (abridged edition). ISBN 92 825 7657 4.	Office for Official Publications of the European Communities	1987	10.60
Single European Act 1986. Cm 372. ISBN 0 10 103722 8.	HMSO		3.80
Treaty on European Union. Cm 1934. ISBN 0 10 119342 4.	HMSO	1992	13.30

Acronyms and Abbreviations

ACP	African, Caribbean and Pacific members of the Lomé Convention
CAP	Common Agricultural Policy
COMETT	Community Action Programme in Education and Training for Technology
EAGGF	European Agricultural Guidance and Guarantee Fund
EBRD	European Bank for Reconstruction and Development
ECSC	European Coal and Steel Community
ECU	European Currency Unit
EDF	European Development Fund
EEA	European Economic Area
EEC	European Economic Community
EFTA	European Free Trade Association
EIB	European Investment Bank
EMS	European Monetary System
EMU	Economic and monetary union
ERASMUS	European Community Action Scheme for the Mobility of University Students
ERDF	European Regional Development Fund
ERM	Exchange rate mechanism
ESF	European Social Fund
ESPRIT	European Strategic Programme for Research and Development in Information Technology
EURATOM	European Atomic Energy Community
GATT	General Agreement on Tariffs and Trade
GSP	Generalised System of Preferences
IMT	Industrial and Materials Technology
MFA	Multi-Fibre Arrangement
NATO	North Atlantic Treaty Organisation
OEEC	Organisation for European Economic Co-operation
RACE	Research and Development in Advanced Communications Technologies in Europe
SPRINT	Strategic Programme for Innovation and Technology Transfer
TEMPUS	Trans-European Mobility Scheme for University Students
WEU	Western European Union

Index

Printed in the UK for HMSO.
Dd 0294517, 11/92, C30, 51-2423, 5673.

A MONTHLY UPDATE

CURRENT AFFAIRS:
A MONTHLY SURVEY

Using the latest authoritative information from official and other sources, *Current Affairs* is an invaluable digest of important developments in all areas of British affairs. Focusing on policy initiatives and other topical issues, its factual approach makes it the ideal companion for *Britain Handbook* and *Aspects of Britain*. Separate sections deal with governmental; international; economic; and social, cultural and environmental affairs. A further section provides details of recent documentary sources for these areas. There is also a twice-yearly index.

Annual subscription including index and postage £35·80 net.
Binder £4·95.

Buyers of Britain 1993: An Official Handbook *qualify for a discount of 25 per cent on a year's subscription to* Current Affairs *(see next page)*.

HMSO Publications Centre
(Mail and telephone orders only)
PO Box 276
LONDON SW8 5DT
Telephone orders: 071 873 9090

THE ANNUAL PICTURE

BRITAIN
1993

AN OFFICIAL HANDBOOK

BRITAIN HANDBOOK

The annual picture of Britain is provided by *Britain: An Official Handbook* - the forty-fourth edition will be published early in 1993. It is the unrivalled reference book about Britain, packed with information and statistics on every facet of British life.

With a circulation of over 20,000 worldwide, it is essential for libraries, educational institutions, business organisations and individuals needing easy access to reliable and up-to-date information, and is supported in this role by its sister publication, *Current Affairs: A Monthly Survey.*

Approx. 500 pages; 24 pages of colour illustrations; 16 maps; diagrams and tables throughout the text; and a statistical section. Price £19·50.

Buyers of Britain 1993: An Official Handbook *have the opportunity of a year's subscription to* Current Affairs *at 25 per cent off the published price of £35·80. They will also have the option of renewing their subscription next year at the same discount. Details in each copy of* Handbook, *from HMSO Publications Centre and at HMSO bookshops (see back of title page).*